INDIA
TORTURE, RAPE & DEATHS IN CUSTODY

AI Index: ASA 20/06/92

ISBN: 0 86210 209 x

First published March 1992

Amnesty International
Publications
1 Easton Street
London WC1X 8DJ
United Kingdom

Printed by:
Flashprint Enterprises Ltd.

Copyright
Amnesty International
Publications

Original language English

All rights reserved

No part of this publication may be reproduced, stored in a retrieval system, or transmitted in any form or by any means electronic, mechanical, photocopying, recording and/or otherwise, without the prior permission of the publishers

CONTENTS

	Introduction	01

1 Torture: patterns and victims — 07
　The pattern of torture — 10
　　Torture of criminal suspects — 12
　　Torture to punish political activism — 13
　　The most vulnerable victims — 14
　Torture in counter-insurgency — 18
　　Jammu and Kashmir — 19
　　Assam and the northeast states — 24
　　Punjab — 29

2 Deaths in custody — 32
　The evidence — 32
　Numbers — 39
　The victims — 41
　　Criminal suspects — 43
　　Minority groups — Muslims — 44
　　Dalits and adivasis — 45
　　Victims of armed conflict — 48

3 Impunity: condoning custodial violence — 55
　Failure to convict — 55
　Legally sanctioned impunity — 59
　Non-legal systems of impunity: systematic cover-up — 61
　　Failure to comply with legal requirements — 61
　　Distortion of cause of death — 65
　　Intimidation of witnesses — 68
　Involvement of magistrates — 71
　Medical aspects of official cover-up — 72

4 Why the police use torture — 76

5 Remedies — 80
　The law — 80
　The practice — 81
　Inquiries — 83
　Compensation — 86
　Civil suits and private criminal complaints — 89

6 A 10 point program to combat torture — 91

Appendix I: A list of 415 deaths in custody in India   101

Appendix II: India: background   194

Appendix III: Amnesty International's work on India   195

INTRODUCTION

"We don't torture anybody. I can be very categorical about that. Wherever we have had complaints of torture we've had it checked and we've not found it to be true". This is what the late Prime Minister of India, Rajiv Gandhi, said in January 1988 when questioned about India's human rights record during an interview on the British television program, *Panorama*.

Yet torture is pervasive and a daily routine in every one of India's 25 states, irrespective of whether arrests are made by the police, the paramilitary forces or the army. It happens regardless of the political persuasion of the party in power. Many hundreds, if not thousands, have died because of torture during the last decade.

This report describes in detail the pattern and practice of torture, including rape, and deaths in custody in India, where Amnesty International has recorded the deaths of 415 people in the custody of the police and security forces since 1985. In all 415 cases there is evidence that the victims, who include women and children, were brutally beaten or otherwise tortured until they died.

The cases described in this report are only a sample of the total (covering most states, plus Delhi); according to the Indian news media, many cases are never reported at all, especially if they occur in remote areas. Reports of deaths in custody are so routine in India that the newspapers simply call them "lock-up deaths". "A discernable pattern in all these police killings, euphemistically called deaths in police lock-up, is that the victims were picked up at random, illegally confined and tortured to extract confessions till they died. Mock post-mortems were conducted and the bodies hurriedly disposed of ", commented the *Indian Express* in October 1986.

INDIA

Half of India's 844 million people are poor and illiterate, and a quarter of them are officially recognized as being in need of special protection. People from this most vulnerable section of the population form the majority of torture victims: members of the scheduled castes and scheduled tribes, tribal women in the northeast, migrant workers, landless labourers. Many who were tortured to death were never charged with any crime: "Senior police officials admit that it is only the 'small fry' who usually die in police custody ... victims are mainly petty offenders while some are innocent"[1]. Other victims are people arrested for their political convictions or people arrested in connection with the situations of armed conflict that prevail in the northeast, Jammu and Kashmir, and Punjab. In the northeast states, and Jammu and Kashmir there is a pattern of rape of women by the army and paramilitary forces for perceived support for armed insurgents. Rape and ill-treatment of women by the police is widespread throughout the country.

Many judges, journalists, lawyers, civil libertarians, writers, politicians, state officials and even police officers themselves, are deeply concerned about the widespread torture, custodial rape and deaths in custody in India. Chief Justice R.S. Pathak, of the Supreme Court of India, said in 1988: "We are gravely concerned at the increasing number of deaths which are reported of persons detained in police lock-ups"[2]. Jyoti Basu, Chief Minister of West Bengal where Amnesty International has recorded 43 deaths allegedly following torture since 1985, proclaimed in October 1987: "Deaths in police custody are unthinkable in any civilised society. It is illegal and absolutely sickening. Nothing could be worse". In March 1990 Upendra Baxi, the Vice Chancellor of Delhi University and a legal expert, commented in the Indian Express: " The practice of third degree by the police has become an ingrained way of law enforcement in India. But widespread practice of torture and terror in the course of daily law enforcement flouts the basic rights recognised by the Indian Constitution and the international instruments on human rights to which India, rightly, is a party". The Indian Government renewed its obligation to protect human rights in October 1991, when the Commonwealth Heads of Government Meeting, which included Prime Minister Narasimha Rao, adopted the Harare Commonwealth Declaration, which reaffirmed the fundamental guiding principles of the Commonwealth and emphasized the commitment to uphold human rights.

Numerous other Indians, notably civil libertarians, have also

INTRODUCTION

persistently urged the government to act to halt police violence against detainees. But successive Indian governments have failed to do so. They chose not to implement a 1985 proposal by the Law Commission that would facilitate the prosecution of those responsible for killing people in custody. Nor have they acted on the many, often excellent, recommendations made over the years by the National Police Commission, such as making judicial inquiries mandatory in all cases of death or grievous injury caused in police custody.

A major cause of the persistence of widespread torture in India is the failure or unwillingness of leading government officials and representatives to acknowledge that torture even exists, let alone that it needs to be vigorously tackled. The government maintains this position despite the fact that judges, journalists, expert commentators, police officers themselves, and official commissions have attested to its widespread occurrence. In response to the 33 specific allegations of torture and deaths in custody raised by the United Nations (UN) Special Rapporteur on torture between 1988 and the end of 1990, the Indian Government either denied them — saying they were "concocted" — provided the police version of events, said the allegations were "under investigation" or failed to give any response even when the allegations had been confirmed in court. Typical is the response India's representative gave to the 42nd session of the UN Sub-Commission on Prevention of Discrimination and Protection of Minorities on 27 August 1990:

"Amnesty has also alleged that torture of detainees continues to be reported from India, resulting in some cases in death. However, it has given no details to substantiate this allegation. The law in India forbids a police officer to use more than the minimum force required to deal with a particular situation. The government has issued directives to police personnel to desist from such methods during investigation and interrogation which can cause torture ... in India an entire network of safeguards within a democratic system are available to prevent the occurrence of human rights violations such as the torture of detainees. These safeguards include a completely free press, public awareness and the institutions of a vibrant and healthy democracy. Despite such safeguards, a few isolated cases of torture of detainees can take place as they can

INDIA

elsewhere in the world ... Whenever allegations of torture are made even in the press, there is a regular investigation by a Judicial Magistrate and if anyone is found remiss in his duty, proper action is taken ... Police personnel found guilty of torturing detainees are liable to receive exemplary punishment."

The facts presented in this report show this is not the case. Section 176 of the Code of Criminal Procedure makes an investigation by a magistrate obligatory in all cases of death in police custody. Yet, despite extensive research which involved Amnesty International writing to all relevant state officials to establish what action they had taken to investigate specific allegations of torture resulting in death, the organization has been able to discover no more than 42 magisterial inquiries conducted in a total of 415 cases. It found that judicial inquiries were ordered in 20 cases. With the notable exception of the high quality judicial investigations sometimes ordered by the Andhra Pradesh government, the full findings of inquiries are rarely published.

Particularly disturbing is the fact that few police officers are ever brought to trial and virtually none are convicted for committing human rights violations. As far as Amnesty International has been able to establish, police officers were arrested in only 25 cases of death in custody which occurred since 1985 and criminal charges were brought in only 52 cases. In no more than three cases are officers known to have been convicted of murdering people in their custody. As *The Statesman* commented in August 1989: "the main reason why barbarous third degree methods are still used, despite being illegal, is that the police know full well that they are [a] protected species and that no harm will come to them if the odd prisoner dies in the lock-up". A senior former official commented: "In India public demonstrations and loud protests in legislatures have to be organised before police officers are punished for their illegal acts. Very often the only action is transfer, followed by the hushing up of the case by superior police officers"[3].

In fact, this report presents extensive evidence that senior police, executive magistrates, doctors and state officials themselves participate in the cover-up of such crimes or shield the police officers responsible from being brought to justice. Commenting on the brutal murder of a farmer in police custody for refusing to pay bribes to a police constable, the chief justice of India's Supreme Court in 1985 found: "Police officers alone and none else can give

INTRODUCTION

evidence regarding the circumstances in which a person in their custody comes to receive injuries. Bound by the ties of brotherhood, they often prefer to remain silent in such situations and when they choose to speak, they put their own gloss upon facts and pervert the truth".

The police are poorly paid, inadequately trained and face unrealistic pressures to produce high "conviction rates". They often respond by torturing suspects: "The pattern of lock-up deaths is only too familiar. A suspect is picked up by the police on a complaint and interrogated. Since the police is supposed to produce the culprit in court within 24 hours of arrest, they need a 'confession' to make their case air-tight. To obtain this, they use time tested third degree methods. Sometimes they go too far and the result is one more lock-up death"[4].

Growing political interference has often turned the police into the agents of the party in power. The pressures which state ruling parties exert on the police, for party political purposes, to provide results at all costs have contributed to and sometimes directly resulted in the police torturing suspects and political opponents, even to death.

Redress for the victims or their families is almost impossible to obtain; most of them have neither the information nor the resources required to seek it. The Armed Forces Special Powers Act, in force in Assam, Jammu and Kashmir and Punjab, states where armed opposition groups are active, grants the security forces immunity from prosecution for "anything done or purported to be done" under the Act. The police are protected from prosecution by the Code of Criminal Procedure for acts committed while on official duty. The government amended the Code of Criminal Procedure in September 1991 to strengthen that protection in states under President's Rule — direct rule from New Delhi[5]. Faced with a failure by the authorities to prosecute, some relatives have brought private complaints. These are hard to substantiate, because most inquiries into custodial deaths, if held at all, are conducted by a member of the civil service and not by an independent authority and reports of these inquiries and of post-mortem examinations are often withheld. Moreover, the police often obstruct inquiries and intimidate witnesses to prevent them from giving evidence. Private criminal prosecutions are costly and subject to extremely long delays.

Whenever relatives have tried to obtain compensation, the

INDIA

Indian Government has argued that it is not responsible for unlawful acts committed by officials on duty. Of the 415 cases listed in Appendix I to this report, compensation was ordered in only 12 cases and is known to have been paid to the families of the victims in only six cases, following protracted legal proceedings. In the case of a student, P. Rajan, who was tortured to death in 1976, the proceedings took no less than 14 years to complete. The police finally conceded in 1990 that Rajan had died in custody. Extraordinary though it may appear, such lengthy delays are not uncommon. As this report shows, they are just one more technique the authorities use to deny redress to victims of human rights violations. Archana Guha, a school-teacher who was paralysed after torture in 1974, has been fighting through the courts since 1977 to bring her torturers to justice, so far without success.

By denying that torture occurs and failing to condemn it, by failing to properly train and provide for the police, by failing to ensure that legal safeguards are adhered to and that proper investigations are conducted into alleged human rights violations, by endorsing and sometimes participating in police and other coverups, by failing to ensure that the guilty are brought to justice, and by failing to adequately compensate the victims, successive Indian governments bear full responsibility for the persistence of widespread torture and rape which cause so many people to die each year in the custody of its law enforcement personnel. Amnesty International believes that the government should now show the political will and determination to change that.

This report shows that many Indians have struggled against great odds to expose torture and to demand accountability. The Indian Government, while refusing access to international organizations and failing to respond seriously to the international human rights procedures of the UN, has claimed that its legal system, free press and civil liberties organizations are adequate to address human rights violations. Sadly this is demonstratively not the case. In an era where it is widely recognized that human rights are an international concern, those struggling for human rights in India need the active support of the international community.

1

Torture: patterns and victims

Torture is not only frequently reported in India, it has even been depicted in newspapers. In May 1991 the *Hindustan Times* published a photograph of a man apparently being tortured in a police station. The caption read: "... Here is Kailash Rai, a suspect, being given the 'aeroplane' treatment by a policeman in Baktiarpur police station.... Kailash bowed before the 'aeroplane' and is reported to have confessed to his being a mercenary hired for booth-capturing in the forthcoming elections in Bihar".

Many torture victims were arrested in connection with criminal investigations and tortured to extract information and confessions. Others were arrested because a relative or friend was sought by the police or because false charges were brought against them at the behest of powerful local interests — members of state ruling parties, businessmen or landowners. This is particularly common in states in which there is organized opposition to economic exploitation, such as Bihar, where the police appear often to act as an instrument of repression on behalf of local ruling groups.

Torture is also widespread in areas where the government faces armed opposition — Jammu and Kashmir, Punjab, Assam and the northeast states — and regions of central India where the *Naxalites* are active. Here torture is a means of obtaining confessions and gathering intelligence, but it has an extra dimension: it is also used as a deterrent and in reprisal for attacks by armed groups.

The most common torture methods are severe beatings, sometimes while the victim is hung upside down, and electric shocks. People have also been crushed with heavy rollers, burned, stabbed with sharp instruments, and had objects such as chilies or thick

INDIA

sticks forced into their rectums. Sexual mutilation has been reported.

Rape is a common form of torture. It is so routine that a 1988 newspaper headline read: "Another mass rape by Bihar cops". In September 1989 the Rajasthan state government admitted that the police had been involved in over 50 rapes in the past few years. According to the Delhi police, 14 cases of rape were reported involving 20 police officers at 12 police stations between 1 January and 11 February 1990. Rape of women appears to be used by the police and the security forces to deter opposition and also as a means of indirectly punishing the men from a particular village or area. As an editorial in *The Statesman* commented, "the police abuse women to carry out a proxy war against what their menfolk stand for".

Almost all Amnesty International's information about torture and death in custody comes from within India itself. Amnesty International has regularly monitored Indian public information sources, including journals and newspapers, during the period covered by this report. The organization has been denied access to India for research purposes by successive governments since 1984: it has nevertheless obtained first-hand information from a variety of sources and evidence contained in medical and judicial records as well as sworn affidavits by the victims and witnesses to torture. Particularly important have been the findings of official commissions of inquiry into aspects of police behaviour and into specific allegations of abuse.

Independent civil liberties organizations have played a crucial role in monitoring and bringing to public attention cases of human rights violations. They have published the results of detailed on-the-spot investigations into torture, rape and death in custody. It is often only as a result of their work that a pattern of human rights violations can be documented, particularly in remote areas. These organizations include the Andhra Pradesh Civil Liberties Committee (APCLC); the Association for the Protection of Democratic Rights (APDR), Calcutta; the Civil Liberties and Human Rights Organization (CLAHRO) in Manipur; Citizens for Democracy (CFD), Delhi; the Committee for the Protection of Democratic Rights (CPDR), Bombay; the Free Legal Aid Committee (FLAC) in Bihar; the Jammu and Kashmir People's Basic Rights (Protection) Committee; the Naga People's Movement for Human Rights (NPMHR); the People's Union for Civil Liberties (PUCL); and

CHAPTER 1

the People's Union for Democratic Rights (PUDR).

Numerous cases of torture have been reported in the Indian news media but these represent only a fraction of the real total. Torture frequently goes unreported unless there is an investigation by an independent human rights or civil liberties body, some form of public protest, or a political dimension. Successive Indian governments have persistently refused to investigate the abuses documented in such reports and have frequently sought to discredit their authors. Some civil liberties activists have been detained because of their work.

In exceptional cases the courts have taken action to prevent torture. The Guwahati High Court, which has jurisdiction over all seven northeast states, has taken significant steps to restrain the army from using torture and committing other human rights violations[6]. In July 1991 the court suspended five police officers from Tripura, accused of torturing detainees, and instructed the director general of police to initiate proceedings against them. The court also ordered the immediate transfer of the officer in charge of the police station where the torture occurred and directed the state government not to confine any prisoners there.

In July 1991 the Supreme Court declared that the army was under a duty to comply strictly with the requirements of the Code of Criminal Procedure when arresting or searching women. This ruling was delivered after newspapers reported that women were being harassed by members of the security forces in the northeast states. Other Supreme Court judgments about female detainees, however, have been openly criticized. For example, in December 1989 the Supreme Court reduced by half the 10-year sentences passed on two police constables in Haryana who had been convicted of rape. The court's ruling was based on its assessment of the victim's character; it provoked much criticism, not least because it appeared to negate a 1983 amendment to the law on rape. This had introduced a minimum sentence of 10 years' imprisonment for any police officer convicted of custodial rape.

Journalists who expose human rights violations have also been detained and ill-treated. Threats against journalists and assaults on them are frequently reported. In July 1989 Bramhadeo Singh Sharma, 84-year-old editor of *Awaaz*, a Hindi newspaper in Bihar, was dragged from his house by police and forced to remain standing for several hours. This occurred after he wrote an editorial condemning the police administration for failing to punish officers who

INDIA

had publicly stripped and beaten unconscious Malati Manjhiyan, a tribal teenage girl. He was released following protests by journalists and others. The seven police officers responsible, including the senior officer, were suspended but no further action is known to have been taken against them.

This case is just one which illustrates official failure to acknowledge that torture occurs. In November 1989 the United Nations (UN) Special Rapporteur on torture[7] transmitted information about the case of Malati Manjhiyan to the Indian Government and sought its response. In January 1990 the Supreme Court had upheld Malati Manjhiyan's claim for compensation and awarded her damages against the police but despite this, the government had still not responded to the UN by the end of 1990. The government's persistent failure to acknowledge that torture is routine serves to ensure that the established pattern of its practice throughout India will continue.

The pattern of torture

In May 1990 the Supreme Court quashed criminal charges against 28 men who had been awaiting trial in Bihar for over 10 years. This is the only case known to Amnesty International in which charges have been dropped against torture victims. It also ordered the release on parole of two others who had been sentenced to 20 years' imprisonment in 1987. The case was one of the best known because of the particularly cruel and inhuman torture inflicted on the accused, victims of the Bhagalpur blindings.

At the end of the 1970s police in Bihar, faced with a steep rise in armed robbery carried out by gangs of young men, decided to blind suspects as a deterrent to others. Over 30 men and boys were deliberately blinded with thick needles and acid between October 1979 and November 1980. The youngest victim was 16 years old. Few of the 30 who were blinded had criminal records and, according to one commentator, no more than four had previously been charged with involvement in criminal activities. One victim, Suresh Sah, was apparently blinded as a punishment for refusing to work for low wages for local landlords. A police sub-inspector, a doctor and eight landlords were convicted in 1984 of a criminal conspiracy to blind him.

The blindings were first reported in the weekly magazine *Sunday* on 16 November 1980 and caused a public outcry. Indira

CHAPTER 1

Gandhi, then Prime Minister, said in parliament: "I want to convey my own deep agony at what has happened.... This is not just a question of punishment, we must make a major effort in the training of these forces whereby they do not become dehumanised". The victims were awarded compensation and rehabilitation and had their trials stayed by the Supreme Court, which immediately ordered medical examination of the victims, asked its own Registrar to investigate the case and asked the courts in Bihar why they had not proceeded against the accused police officers. The court ordered the Bihar state government to produce all relevant documents to clarify the involvement of state officials in the blindings. The Bihar government sought to disclaim responsibility on the grounds that its officers had acted outside the law.

The man who had been instrumental in exposing the blindings was the superintendent of Bhagalpur jail. He was suspended without pay in December 1980 for allegedly not revealing the full facts of the case. Yet, according to his petition to the Supreme Court appealing against his suspension, he had first reported the blinding of a prisoner in November 1979, when he sent a report to the chief judicial magistrate, urging him to carry out an investigation. He said that he had repeatedly notified the authorities that prisoners awaiting trial in Bhagalpur jail had been deliberately blinded by the police. He said that he had taken the inspector general of prisons to interview three of the blinded prisoners but that the inspector general's subsequent demands for a full inquiry were ignored.

The superintendent also said that the home commissioner, the Bihar minister for jails and other state officials were aware of the blindings but had made no attempt to prevent or investigate them. "In spite of the best possible efforts made by me as well as by...the then Inspector General of Prisons, Bihar, to bring the matter to the notice of the appropriate authorities so that they might take steps to prevent the recurrence of blindings, I found the local authorities as well as the state government insensitive towards the blinded and by now 31 suspects had been blinded."

The first inquiry was carried out by the deputy inspector general of the Bihar Criminal Investigation Department (CID). He was ordered to go to Bhagalpur to establish whether the police had carried out the blindings. He later said: "I was given the job because they knew that I had a great weakness for the police force...and they expected me to cover up. I went thinking that the police could never be guilty of such brutality, but after examining the victims for two

INDIA

days I got 32 cases instituted against 10 police officers". When his superiors received his first report, he alleged, his inquiries were promptly blocked. Nevertheless, he submitted a 70-page report to the Bihar government in December 1980, followed in January 1981 by separate reports on each case. On 10 February 1981 he was told to vacate his office by the following day and was demoted.

The next inquiry, carried out by the Central Bureau of Investigation (CBI) in January 1982, absolved the state government of complicity or negligence in the blindings. It found that they were isolated instances of crime without any conspiracy and recommended criminal prosecution in 10 cases, and departmental action in a further nine cases. The cases against the police officers proceeded very slowly through the courts. According to Amnesty International's information, the last case was heard in 1987. In all, nine police officers were convicted for their part in blinding just five of the prisoners. No senior officer was prosecuted, although the CBI had reported that at least one had prior knowledge of the blindings and did not act to prevent them.

The police blindings in Bhagalpur illustrate key aspects of the pattern of torture in India: the sanction of torture by state and local judicial authorities, the routine concealment of torture, the failure to conduct proper inquiries, and the inordinate length of judicial proceedings — it was 10 years after the blindings that the Supreme Court quashed the charges against the victims. However, the case is exceptional because a nationwide public outcry resulted in concern at the highest level of government and the prosecution and punishment of at least some of those responsible. Nevertheless, several of the police officers allegedly involved apparently escaped trial and the longest sentence served by a police officer convicted of deliberately blinding a prisoner was three years.

Torture of criminal suspects

Criminal suspects form a large proportion of India's torture victims. The most common purpose of torturing criminal suspects is to extract a confession, or to secure information about a crime, however petty the offence and irrespective of whether a crime has actually been committed. In April 1989 the Bombay High Court ordered a police investigation into the torture of four teenage girls by the Maharashtra police. The four girls, all members of a nomadic tribe, had been charged with "moving about in a suspicious manner". Many victims of torture are jobless, slum-dwellers or migrant labourers who have come to the cities in search of work.

CHAPTER 1

Most victims of police rape in Delhi, for example, are migrant women, who often disappear after the rape because they are too frightened to pursue the matter.

Even children as young as six have been arrested and tortured in connection with petty criminal offences. In mid-1989 the press reported that a group of children and teenagers had been tortured in northwest Delhi. The children, all slum-dwellers, were detained on 26 June 1989 on suspicion of theft. The case was brought to public attention by two civil liberties groups, which reported that 11 children, including two 10-year-old girls and a boy aged six, had been illegally detained and tortured throughout the night. A girl of 13 had been stripped naked and beaten and one 12-year-old boy was given electric shocks and beaten with a leather belt; another boy was stripped, hung upside-down from the ceiling and beaten unconscious. The children were released the following day after a crowd of 4,000 people had gathered outside the police station.

Lawyers successfully petitioned the courts for the children to be given a medical examination. The publicity this case received forced the police to announce an inquiry, although the deputy commissioner of police denied that the police were responsible. He said the children had been "roughed up" by members of the family whose goods were stolen. The case was the subject of an inquiry to the Indian Government by the UN Special Rapporteur on torture and it was cited in his 1989 report[8], but as of the end of 1990 the government had not responded.

Torture to punish political activism
There is also a pattern of torture and ill-treatment in punitive reprisals for resistance to police or military operations. In many Indian states the police have been accused of detaining and torturing people on false charges at the behest of influential local interests. For example, the Calcutta-based *Telegraph* reported in February 1990 that villagers from Rampur village, near Balagarh in West Bengal, said they had been tortured due to pressure from local members of the state ruling party, the Communist Party of India (Marxist). Apparently, a CPI(M) activist had lodged a false complaint of assault against a village leader who was a member of the rival Congress(I) party. The police then took a number of villagers, including several women, into custody and reportedly tortured them at Balagarh police station: one victim was a 12-year-old girl, Sabina Yasmeen. Another victim, Sheikh Abdul Wal, alleged: "The police beat me up black and blue saying I must not

dare to support the Congress again". The local deputy superintendent of police denied the allegations.

In early September 1991 a Delhi policewoman was among several men and women detained and tortured after police raided the village of Barhi in Ballabgarh, Haryana. The raid was apparently in reprisal for an incident on 30 August, when police officers attempting to arrest villagers in connection with a land dispute were reportedly stoned and beaten. Four days later a force of some 100 police officers armed with *lathis*[9] and guns attacked the village. Villagers were reportedly beaten indiscriminately and their property destroyed.

According to policewoman constable, Neelkamal, who was visiting relatives in the village, "They just broke open the front door and rushed inside. My two sisters-in-law were beaten up and dragged outside by the police. When I told them I am also in the police, they just smirked and said 'so what?', and started beating me up. They then dragged me outside and took me to the village school building where villagers were also rounded up. We were then taken to the police station. Here they started beating us once again and forcibly stripped our menfolk"[10].

Twenty-nine women, five men and a 13-year-old boy were reportedly subjected to this treatment. Fourteen villagers were subsequently charged by the police with rioting and attempted murder. The incident provoked widespread protests throughout the state. On 5 September the Haryana chief minister announced a judicial inquiry. He acknowledged that police excesses had occurred, but denied allegations that village men had been forcibly stripped and paraded before the women. He announced the suspension of one police officer and the transfer of another.

The most vulnerable victims

Many Indians are members of the scheduled castes (castes which are recognized by the constitution as oppressed), or members of the scheduled tribes, known as *adivasis*. The term *dalit*[11] — meaning "oppressed" — has been used to describe militant members of the scheduled castes. It has now gained broader currency and Amnesty International uses it in its broadest sense to describe all members of the scheduled castes, not merely the most militant.

Dalits and *adivasis* are the poorest and most vulnerable groups of people in India. Their special vulnerability has been recognized as requiring extra protection, notably in the Indian Constitution, Article 17 of which forbids untouchability and its practice in any

CHAPTER 1

form, and in the 1955 Untouchability Offences Act (which was retitled the Civil Rights Protection Act in 1976).

The Scheduled Castes and the Scheduled Tribes (Prevention of Atrocities) Act was passed in September 1989, making illegal some 24 social and economic abuses of the scheduled groups. The Act makes it a criminal offence for legal and administrative proceedings to be deliberately abused by police or security forces in cases involving members of scheduled groups. It allows states to establish special courts to try such cases and provides for legal aid and for compensation for victims of abuse.

Since this legislation was passed, however, human rights violations against *dalits* and *adivasis* have persisted, and police are frequently reported culpable. In May 1990 the then Prime Minister, V.P. Singh, stated in parliament that his government would take the "sternest action" against those involved in violations against members of the scheduled groups. However, this and similar official statements have not resulted in an appreciable increase in the judicial investigation and prosecution of police officers involved in such offences. Not one special court was known to have been established under the Act by October 1991.

In June 1990 a public outcry forced the Maharashtra state government to suspend several police officers and order a police inquiry into the killing of a teenage nomadic tribal youth and the torture of his pregnant sister. The boy, Namdeo Atak, was reportedly beaten to death for trying to prevent seven police officers abducting and raping his sister, Parvati Rusankote. According to Parvati Rusankote, "They were all drunk and were dressed in ordinary clothes. They ordered me to come with them. I refused. Then they began abusing me and two of them lifted me by my hands and feet". When Namdeo Atak insisted on accompanying his sister, he was also thrown into their jeep. Both were taken to the Tulzapur police station. Here, according to Parvati Rusankote: "Some of the seven policemen tied Namdeo to a table and began whipping him with their belts and hitting him with their *lathis*. Meanwhile, the rest caught hold of me. One of them gripped my hair and ripped apart my blouse, while another disrobed me and stood on my thighs.... They kept abusing me and also kicked me on the stomach".

Namdeo Atak was beaten unconscious. He and his sister were then taken back to their home where Namdeo Atak was beaten again in front of his father. Parvati Rusankote says that her brother died

INDIA

after four hours of beating: "The policemen left only when they were certain he was dead". A medical examination of Namdeo Atak's body reportedly found some 40 external injuries and many broken bones. However, the Maharashtra chief minister rejected calls for a judicial inquiry into the case.

Women are singled out for special protection under the Scheduled Castes and Scheduled Tribes Act; sexual assault of the women of the scheduled groups is an offence, as is their sexual exploitation by people in a "dominant position". However, police rape of *dalit* and *adivasi* women continues to be widely reported. In August 1991 the Bihar state government announced an inquiry, headed by a senior female police officer, into allegations that police had raped villagers in Chaksoagpur, Muzaffarpur district, in July.

Dalits and *adivasis* are frequently tortured for political reasons, to deter them or punish them for involvement in organized resistance to economic exploitation. Often *adivasi* and *dalit* villages have been raided, and their inhabitants tortured and raped, by police acting in collusion with local ruling groups, such as landowners. Such abuses are common in Bihar, where most torture victims are landless labourers and their families campaigning for land reform and minimum wages. Landlords have often resorted to violence to suppress such campaigns with the assistance of criminal gangs or private armies, whose growth is believed to have been encouraged by the police since the late 1970s. In a number of cases local police officers are alleged to have cooperated with such groups or even participated in attacks on landless people.

In May 1988, 23 women from Majhua village, Purnea District, were raped by police during a raid on the village, reportedly instigated by a local contractor as part of an attempt to intimidate villagers who had refused to work for less than the minimum wage. The police were armed and reportedly responded to any resistance with violence. The rape victims were said to include an 80-year-old woman, and a baby girl, aged one, was reportedly molested.

The police are said to have maintained a 24-hour guard on the village to prevent publicity about the incident and a journalist who tried to publish a report on the incident in a local newspaper was threatened with death. The district magistrate, said by some to be a friend of the contractor allegedly involved, denied the rapes had occurred and dismissed the allegations as fabricated by "criminal elements" in Majhua. When women from the village assembled to protest in Purnea, they were dispersed by the police with *lathis*.

CHAPTER 1

Forty million *adivasis*, 85 per cent of India's total tribal population, inhabit the resource rich lands that stretch across central India. Most of them live below the poverty line; their rate of literacy is one-third of the national average. Economic development in the region, including forestry, mining and hydro-electric projects, has resulted in increasing numbers of tribal peoples losing their traditional homes and livelihoods. Many now seek a living as small farmers, or as agricultural labourers working for large landowners, while others migrate to the cities in search of work.

In recent years tribal protests have centred on the questions of compensation for land lost to their communities, the distribution of surplus land, low wages, and autonomy for tribal regions. These demands have been supported by left-wing political groups, some of which — such as the Maoist revolutionaries known as *Naxalites* — have engaged in violent opposition to the authorities, particularly in Andhra Pradesh, Madhya Pradesh and Maharashtra. In an effort to crush such opposition, police have carried out widespread arrests and torture of adivasis suspected of involvement in such protests.

The *Naxalites* became active in the Bastar district of Madhya Pradesh, where the majority of the population are tribal peoples, in the early 1980s. In addition to organizing strikes and other forms of protest, the *Naxalites* carried out attacks on the police and murdered landowners and other civilians. In 1985 the state of Madhya Pradesh was declared a "disturbed area" under the Terrorist and Disruptive Activities (Prevention) Act (TADA). The strength of the civil police force in Bastar has been doubled in the past decade and several companies of armed police attached to the Madhya Pradesh Special Armed Force (SAF) are deployed in the district.

In July 1989 the PUCL issued a report on the situation in Bastar[12]. The PUCL had investigated the pattern behind an estimated 90 armed police raids on *adivasi* villages since the imposition of the TADA. The report stated: "A large contingent of armed police sometimes as many as 100 descend on a village.... They conduct indiscriminate beatings.... This May [1989] the police took three youths and buried them neck deep in the fields. After such violence the people, especially men, are taken to a police station. There the civil police take over.... They may hang the *adivasis* upside-down from the ceiling, or subject them to the infamous roller treatment and beat them up for days together".

The PUCL concluded: "many people suggest that the *adivasis*

INDIA

are being punished for giving food and shelter to the *Naxalites*. The ostensible purpose of the more sustained interrogations is to find the whereabouts of [the *Naxalites*]. The practice of using abominable third degree methods to extract information from the suspects is perhaps fairly common in most of the police stations of the country. But in Bastar it has absolutely no point since most policemen do not understand the language of the *adivasis* whom they torture".

In June 1991 the PUDR published a report[13] of its investigation of police behaviour in the tribal village of Hadmatiya in Udaipur district, Rajasthan. In March 1990, according to this report, a local large landowner had lodged a complaint of trespass and theft against 37 villagers after they attempted to grow crops in a tank-bed to which they held traditional rights. The complaint was investigated by 11 police officers who visited the village on 5 March and reportedly provoked a riot by mistreating *adivasi* women. Several police officers were beaten. The police withdrew and filed charges of assault and attempted murder against the villagers. Some four weeks later, they also took direct reprisals. According to the PUDR, 14 jeeps, four trucks and a bus load of police officers, accompanied by some of the landowner's agents, surrounded the village and herded the villagers into a field. They then opened fire on the villagers, injuring 35. The women were stripped and beaten. The PUDR concluded that the purpose was to intimidate and terrorize the villagers for opposing the exploitative practices of landowners.

Torture in counter-insurgency

Torture is common in those areas where there are political groups actively seeking independence or increased autonomy, especially when such demands are made by armed opposition groups. These groups are active particularly in Jammu and Kashmir, Punjab and the northeast states. In these areas, armed opponents of the government have been responsible for numerous human rights abuses, including torture, killing and hostage-taking, acts which Amnesty International condemns.

In these areas of armed opposition the security forces are empowered under the Terrorist and Disruptive Activities (Prevention) Act (TADA) to arrest suspects and detain them for up to one year without charge or trial for investigation into broadly defined offences. Detainees held under the TADA are usually denied bail.

CHAPTER 1

They must be tried *in camera*. During the trial the identity of witnesses can be kept secret and the accused is presumed guilty in four situations specified in the TADA.

Jammu and Kashmir

"I yesterday discharged a patient, aged 18-20, who had been in this hospital for three months. Twenty per cent or more of his body had suffered deep burns from a hot clothes-iron. These burns were...so serious that I and other doctors had only just succeeded in saving his life.... He had also been shot by a bullet in the armpit. His torturing with the clothes-iron had all been done during interrogation by the regular army at Sopor".

This statement from a doctor interviewed in a Srinagar hospital in December 1990 is typical of numerous reports of torture received from Jammu and Kashmir since late 1989, when the security forces were given increased powers following mounting violence in the state by armed opposition groups.

More recently, Manzoor Ahmed Naikoo, a shopkeeper filmed in his hospital bed, accused the army of torturing him, telling his interviewer: "After tying me down, they removed my pyjamas. They tied some cloth round my penis and set it on fire.... Then they laid me face down. One man stood on my back. Another brought a rod and inserted it deep through my rectum. He kept thrusting it forward and back". Muzzaffar Shah told a similar story. He also had ruptured intestines, liver and lungs. In the same film, made by the Indian video company, *Eyewitness*, army commander Lieutenant General S. Nath denied their allegations: "There is no torture. We have given very strict orders to our interrogators that they will not use any third degree methods". In November 1991 the government banned the film, citing "military security reasons".

Control over the territory of Kashmir, two-thirds of which constitutes the Indian state of Jammu and Kashmir, has been disputed between India and Pakistan since 1947, leading twice to war between the two countries. Jammu and Kashmir is the only Indian state in which Muslims constitute a majority of the population. The activities of armed Muslim militants seeking the state's independence from India have spread in recent years. Militant armed groups in the state have increasingly resorted to violence and extortion, and have taken, and sometimes killed, hostages. As a result, thousands of Hindus have fled the valley and live in camps

INDIA

in Jammu, the southern part of the state.

In response to this violence, Jammu and Kashmir was placed under President's Rule in July 1990. The Armed Forces Special Powers Act, which provides the security forces with immunity from prosecution[14], was imposed a month later. Since then, Indian security forces have been engaged in a major counter-insurgency operation against armed secessionist and fundamentalist groups and reports of torture and deaths in custody have increased dramatically.

Widespread human rights violations in the state since January 1990 have been attributed to the Indian army, and the paramilitary Border Security Force (BSF) and Central Reserve Police Force (CRPF). A 145,000-strong force of the CRPF was flown into the state at that time. Cordon-and-search operations are frequently conducted in areas of armed opposition activity or after attacks on the security forces, with districts being sealed off and house-to-house searches conducted. Torture is reported to be routinely used during these combing operations as well as in army camps, interrogation centres, police stations and prisons. Indiscriminate beatings are common and rape in particular appears to be routine.

It is impossible to gauge the true extent of torture in Jammu and Kashmir. In July 1991 unofficial sources estimated that 15,000 people were being detained without trial in the state. Many of those detained since late 1989 have alleged after release that they were tortured or ill-treated in custody. In November 1991 Dr Kazi Massrat, the chief casualty officer at the Medical College Hospital, Srinagar, told a British journalist: "I must have treated 250 torture victims in the last year". He said they included men who had been forced to drink large quantities of fluid after having their penises tied tightly. Earlier, in June 1990, recently released villagers from the community of Haihama-Payerpora, Kupwara District, told another British journalist how they had been tortured while detained by the Indian army. When interviewed they still bore massive bruises, burns from electrodes and heated rods, cuts and rope sores. "One man, whose feet were bandaged up to the ankles, said a bed of coal had been covered with corrugated iron and a deep layer of sand, which slowed their progress when the prisoners were forced to run across it...". All had been released without charge after soldiers reportedly threatened to detain and torture them again if they should support the armed opposition.

Detailed information about torture and the victims is hard to

CHAPTER 1

obtain. Access to interrogation and detention centres run by the security forces is restricted even for lawyers. Most torture testimonies come from villagers tortured during counter-insurgency raids, or from former detainees. The Srinagar bench of the Jammu and Kashmir High Court has been inundated with *habeas corpus* petitions of behalf of detainees at risk of torture — 3,000 petitions, according to the court's former Chief Justice in an interview in December 1990, most of which had not been heard.

Information is made even harder to obtain by the strict control the security forces exercise over freedom of movement and freedom of expression. Victims are known to have written to Amnesty International, but none of their letters have reached the organization. Curfews are in force for long periods throughout the area, road blocks and check points policed by the security forces control all movement. Press censorship has been sporadically imposed. Some local newspapers have been banned and their offices sealed. International human rights organizations are also barred. Nevertheless, lawyers, civil liberties groups, and journalists have documented a consistent pattern of torture.

In Jammu and Kashmir, rape is practised as part of a systematic attempt to humiliate and intimidate the local population during counter-insurgency operations. In May 1990 Mubina Gani, a teen-age bride, was detained at a roadblock and raped by BSF soldiers on her way from the marriage ceremony to her husband's home. Her aunt, who was seven months pregnant, was also raped. The official explanation was that the wedding party had been caught in crossfire between two paramilitary units. The victims said that soldiers had fired on them without warning at the roadblock, killing one man and wounding several others before raping the two women. Mubina Gani told one reporter: "We were crying bitterly. I told them I had not yet seen my husband. But they didn't listen.... Four to six persons raped me, I think".

This incident, when it was reported, captured the attention of both the Indian and international press. As a result an inquiry was instigated by the police, and a report from one senior police officer confirmed that the rapes had occurred. However, those responsible have not been brought to justice.

International publicity may also have been the reason why, in June 1991, the army invited a team from the Press Council[15] of India to visit Kunan Poshpora, a village in the district of Kupwara, close to the Line of Control which separates Indian-held Kashmir from

INDIA

Pakistan. Three months earlier, over 20 women had reportedly been raped when soldiers raided the village. The youngest victim was a girl of 13 named Misra, the oldest victim, named Jana, was aged 80.

Kunan Poshpora was raided on the night of 23-24 February 1991 during counter-insurgency operations by soldiers of the 4th Rajput Rifles. Local residents allege that several hundred soldiers arrived at the village at about 11pm, cordoned it off and began house-to-house searches. Many men from the village were taken away and interrogated, in some cases under torture, about the activities of armed opposition groups. At the same time at least 23 women were reportedly raped in their homes at gunpoint. Some are said to have been gang-raped, others to have been raped in front of their children.

The incident was investigated by several different officials. A district magistrate, shocked by the allegations, concluded that there was sufficient evidence to warrant a full inquiry. The army strenuously denied the allegations of rape and torture and appointed an army brigadier to conduct an inquiry. He dismissed the allegations of rape as "malicious and untrue". On 18 March the divisional commissioner visited Kunan Poshpora: he reportedly recommended that a judicial inquiry be established to investigate the incident. A two-member team from the Press Council of India visited Kunan Poshpora for one day, following which it dismissed the statements of at least nine alleged rape victims because of what it described as inconsistencies. Medical evidence, which may have indicated rape, was described as "worthless".

The Indian Government has invoked the results of these inquiries in justification of its claim that rape did not occur. However, the government has withheld the medical findings on the Kunan Poshpura victims included in the Press Council's report and the findings of the inquiry conducted by the divisional commissioner have not been published. His reported recommendation that there should be a thorough investigation is not known to have been implemented.

Lawyers, journalists and others who have attempted to address human rights violations have been detained and tortured or ill-treated. Zahid Ali, a lawyer, was interrogated in the Gupkar Joint Interrogation Centre in Srinagar and reportedly forced under torture to confess to crimes he had not committed. He was apparently detained because of his work on behalf of political detainees. In June 1991 The Telegraph, Calcutta, reported that Noor Al Qamarain, a reporter for the *Kashmir Times*, had been detained for several days and questioned under torture about links between journalists and opposition groups.

People taken into custody for interrogation about armed opposition activities and those associated with such groups face more sustained torture than that meted out during counter-insurgency operations. The methods reported are brutal. In September 1991 a British journalist gave the following description of a torture victim he had seen in a Srinagar hospital. The victim was a villager from Chowki Bal, near the Line of Control, who had been detained and interrogated for three months by the BSF on suspicion of being a guerrilla. "A doctor lifted away [the] sheet gingerly, as though he were removing a huge bandage covering the body's length. Two scars ran parallel from his ribs to his groin. 'We sewed him up,' said [the doctor], who wished to remain unidentified. 'The Indian security forces burnt open his stomach with a clothes iron and then jumped on him with their boots.' [The victim] had lost 60lb in the months in which his captors burned him, skewered him and applied electrodes to his penis."[16]

A young man interviewed in a Srinagar hospital said that he had been tortured during interrogation for two weeks in August 1990: "My armpits were burned by candles.... I was branded by hot irons on the upper arm, my stomach was burned by candles.... My penis was penetrated and punctured by needles. I was also tortured by electric shocks, and cigarette stubs".

The roller treatment — crushing bones with heavy rollers — is reported to be a particularly agonizing torture. A detainee released after eight weeks' interrogation witnessed it inflicted on a boy: "... a big long wooden log was rolled over his body from neck to foot by five men pushing down on it with all their strength. They broke bones and knees and crushed joints. The screams were terrible".

Although the government has announced inquiries, criminal charges and, in some cases, courts martial, Amnesty International knows of only two cases in which members of the paramilitary forces have been charged with offences constituting human rights violations. In the majority of cases, official inquiries have been conducted by the security forces themselves. Where the outcome is known, these inquiries have generally exonerated the security force personnel implicated. The minister of home affairs said in November 1991 that 50 members of the security forces had been suspended, and some imprisoned for human rights violations.

INDIA

However, Amnesty International knows of no cases in which members of the security forces have been convicted of torturing prisoners.

Assam and the northeast states
More than 220 hill tribes live in seven states in northeast India: Assam, Nagaland, Manipur, Arunachal Pradesh, Meghalaya, Mizoram and Tripura. They are ethnically, economically and socially different from inhabitants of other parts of India, from which the northeast is nearly cut off by Bangladesh.

Accusing the central government of neglect and exploitation, several tribal organizations in the northeastern states have advocated autonomy or independence and some have taken up arms in pursuit of these aims. Members of the security forces were first posted to the northeast Indian states in the 1950s. Widespread human rights violations have been attributed to the army, particularly the Assam Rifles, who report directly to the central government's Home and Defence Ministries and, to a lesser extent, to paramilitary forces and the police.

The most serious abuses have been reported from the areas where armed groups such as the National Socialist Council of Nagaland (NSCN), the People's Liberation Army of Manipur, the United Liberation Front of Manipur, and the United Liberation Front of Assam (ULFA), are active. The latter, notably, have captured and even killed hostages. All these organizations are banned. Torture and ill-treatment occur routinely during counter-insurgency operations to flush out suspected members and supporters of these groups.

President's Rule was imposed in Assam on 28 November 1990, in response to a rising level of political violence. The state was declared a "disturbed area" and responsibility for maintaining order was given to the army. The ULFA was banned and a major counter-insurgency offensive — "Operation Bajrang" — was launched. During this campaign, widespread human rights violations were reported. In January 1991 the *Times of India* reported: "Every single day reports pour in from different parts of the state about army atrocities, including killings, torture, rape and harassment.... The local newspapers are full of heart-rending reports of ordinary people being picked up by the army for no reason, women being raped and houses raided at uncanny hours".

Women and girls continue to be raped. On 6 October 1991 Raju Baruah, a girl from Sutargaon, was raped by four soldiers and her

CHAPTER 1

body thrown into a pond. Her sisters identified the soldiers allegedly responsible and the inquest report confirmed signs of rape. Her family was granted Rs 100,000 compensation but it is not known if the soldiers were brought to justice.

Between 28 November and 10 April 1991, when it suspended counter-insurgency operations, the army reportedly arrested 1,846 people in their search for ULFA militants. A further 1,000 were reportedly arrested by the police. Many were detained at random during mass raids on their villages; others were arrested at the army check posts or because they had broken curfew. They included peasants, labourers, academics, political and social activists, doctors, and businessmen. Youths and students were a particular target. Many of those arrested are believed to have been tortured. In December 1990, the army denied allegations of torture and rape during "Operation Bajrang", and claimed they were fabricated by "political leaders with vested interests"[17].

Over 100 *habeas corpus* petitions were filed in the Guwahati High Court between 27 November 1990 and March 1991 on behalf of people illegally detained and tortured during army operations in Assam. The High Court has upheld many petitions and ordered that the detainees be brought before it. Two brothers, Rituraj and Padmaraj Barua, who were detained by the army on 1 and 2 December 1990, both claimed they had been severely tortured for 20 days when the army produced them on the order of the court. The court ordered that they be taken to the Guwahati Medical College hospital for treatment, and transferred them to judicial custody. It awarded the brothers compensation for the torture they had suffered and eventually, on 4 April, released them on bail.

However, the security forces have defied some High Court rulings. In January 1991 the Guwahati High Court acquitted student Rajumoni Bezbarooah and ordered that he not be taken into custody without the permission of the university hostel warden. Rajumoni Bezbarooah was detained again some two months later and reportedly severely tortured at an army camp at Golaghat. He alleged that soldiers had destroyed the court's order when he showed it to them.

Civil liberties organizations have played an important role in documenting human rights violations in Assam. In February 1991 a team from the CPDR visited six districts in Assam. They gathered information on 49 cases of torture, 13 of rape, eight extrajudicial executions and one "disappearance"[18]. The PUDR also published a report on Assam, in May 1991[19]. It concluded: "Most of the persons detained by the army were tortured.... We have interviewed many torture victims, visited three hospitals, met concerned doctors and gone through a number of court documents.

"Beating, stripping and hanging them upside down and then beating on head and chest, thumping on chests with boots, pouring ice cold water, burying them up to chest and then beating or keeping a bucket over the head, squeezing testicles with clamps, dipping in cold water drums, forcefully keeping them awake for days together, denial of food or water are some of the forms of torture used. But the most common form is electric shocks. Sensitive parts of the body including ears, tongue, armpits, genitals and head were repeatedly given electric shocks sometimes in progressively higher voltages. With electrodes at each temple the brain was subjected to electric waves."

An earlier campaign for tribal autonomy in Assam was launched in March 1987 by a tribal association, the All-Bodo Students' Union (ABSU). The campaign began with strikes and demonstrations but increasingly involved bombings, arson attacks and killings of targeted individuals. The Assam Armed Police were sent into Bodo-inhabited areas of the state with orders to deal firmly with the campaign, and Bodo districts were placed under the TADA.

There have since been numerous reports of the torture and killing of Bodo civilians and hundreds have been arbitrarily detained. Amnesty International has details of the alleged torture of 80 Bodos arrested between February 1988 and November 1989. The youngest was an illiterate 12-year-old boy arrested during a raid on his village, Lailang Para, in Darrang district, in September 1989. The methods of torture described range from beatings and asphyxiation to being crushed with heavy rollers and subjected to mock execution.

Rape and ill-treatment of Bodo women by the police and the security forces have also been widely reported. Rape often occurs during raids on villages in search of tribal militants. In March 1989, 15 tribal girls were reportedly raped at Rupnathpur, Kokrajhar district, by members of the Assam Police Task Force (APTF) who had raided the village. At the end of June two Bodo girls, 10-year-old Binati Nable and Aswani Brahan, aged 15, of Goyvari village in Kokrajhar district were gang-raped by police officers during a raid.

CHAPTER 1

Both girls were examined the same day by a doctor at Banargaon, who said he was not authorised to give a report. At the instigation of the All Assam Tribal Women Welfare Association a complaint was lodged the next day with the local police superintendent. An examination of the two girls at Kokrajhar hospital confirmed that they had been subjected to sexual intercourse. The police were informed but no action appears to have been taken.

In Manipur state, hundreds of villagers in and around Oinam were detained and tortured in July 1987 during "Operation Bluebird", ostensibly conducted to search for NSCN members who had earlier attacked a military outpost. Over 300 villagers were interrogated and beaten — some of them so severely that their limbs were broken — given electric shocks, burned with cigarettes or hung upside-down. Pregnant women were beaten and some had miscarriages as a result[20]. Some villagers had chili powder inserted into sensitive parts of their bodies. Others were buried up to their necks and led to believe they would be killed[21]. The youngest victim was one year old, the oldest a man of 65. Thirty-four were children aged 12 and under. Boys of 15 and 16 were tortured with electric shocks.

Local civil liberties lawyers worked hard to ensure that the victims received redress. On 6 June 1988 the Guwahati High Court directed the Imphal Sessions Court to record first-hand evidence from the villagers about the incident. The sessions court concluded its hearings on 21 April 1990. The case is now pending before the Guwahati High Court. Throughout the hearings the security forces have repeatedly attempted to intimidate witnesses and their relatives through illegal detention, torture and death threats. Some of the villagers were arrested by the Assam Rifles and tortured to make them retract their evidence. Others were arrested after they had testified in court. The UN Special Rapporteur on torture, asking the Indian Government about this, was told that these reports were false and politically motivated.

The victims are not only waiting for redress some four years later, but many reportedly still suffer from the effects of torture. The Naga Doctors' Forum and the Drug Action Forum of West Bengal examined 104 of the villagers. According to their August 1990 report, all but three of the villagers were found to be mentally unwell and many still suffered pain and disability from injuries inflicted by torture. Despite the gravity of this incident and the detailed allegations of human rights violations, some of which were confirmed in court, the central government refused to order an independent

INDIA

investigation into the allegations. Only a local police inquiry was held, which confirmed some torture allegations.

Of the armed struggles for local autonomy in northeast India, the Naga insurgency is the oldest. Since 1947 the 1.2 million people of Nagaland have been policed by some 150,000 Indian troops. In October 1990 troops unleashed what one newspaper, *The Hill Express*, described as "a reign of terror" after NSCN guerrillas ambushed an army patrol near Botsa, killing three soldiers and injuring several others. In an apparent attempt to root out NSCN members, the Assam Rifles conducted raids on several villages. According to press reports, villagers were beaten with fists, sticks and rifle butts and tortured by having chili powder rubbed in their eyes and water forced up their nostrils. The victims included a man of 65 who was paralysed and Shri Neo, a villager who had been deaf and mute since birth. Both were reportedly beaten because they were unable to answer soldiers' questions. Over 30 people required hospital treatment for injuries suffered during these raids.

Amnesty International has received affidavits sworn by 16 of the victims. Shri Keveikuolie, a 28-year-old man from Narhema village, gave the following description of his treatment: "Two slapped me while the third held me by my hair. As soon as I fell down, five to six started kicking and hitting me with their rifle butts and barrels all over my body. They then took me to the side of the road and propped me against the wall. I could not stand and I fell down. They then put the barrel of a rifle inside my mouth and asked me either to speak or die".

Rape by the security forces is one of the most frequently reported human rights violations in Tripura state, where the Tripura National Liberation Front (later renamed the Tribal National Front) has resorted to killings and kidnappings in pursuit of its demand for increased rights for Tripura's tribal population. In April 1989 opposition members of the state assembly alleged that there had been 100 cases of rape by the security forces in the previous few months.

Rape usually occurs during counter-insurgency operations and gang-rapes of tribal women by members of the police force and soldiers are frequently reported. In June 1988 the Assam Rifles conducted a cordon-and- search operation in Ujan Maidan, Khowai district, in pursuit of members of the outlawed Tripura National Volunteers. At least 14 tribal women said they were raped during the search and were admitted to Khowai government hospital, one

CHAPTER 1

woman said that her husband had been tied up. The youngest victim was 12 years old. The state government dismissed the allegations but admitted that some women might have been beaten. An inquiry conducted by the police and Assam Rifles found that one woman had "probably" been raped and that two others could have been molested, but no independent investigation was conducted.

In June 1991, 14 tribal women from Gachipara village in Tripura's Dharma Nagar district were dragged from their huts and raped by police officers, while the men were herded into a corner of the village.

Punjab

Thousands of people have been arrested by police and security forces in Punjab since 1983, when armed Sikh opposition groups emerged demanding an independent Sikh state (*Khalistan*). These groups have been responsible for widespread abuses, including the deliberate and arbitrary killing of thousands of civilians, bombings, hostage-takings and assassinations. President's Rule was imposed on Punjab in March 1987.

People have often been arrested on mere suspicion that they are linked to armed Sikh groups or have information about them. Prisoners have been kept detained for months or years without trial under the provisions of special legislation suspending normal legal safeguards. Torture is widespread. Parents, brothers or sisters of suspects have also been arbitrarily detained and tortured in order to extract information about their relatives' whereabouts or activities. Those tortured include young people and the elderly. In May 1991 Amnesty International published a report on human rights violations in Punjab[22]. The Indian Government responded by providing information about 24 of the 42 cases of torture and other human rights violations listed in the report, in most cases denying they had occurred. In a response to the government in August 1991[23], Amnesty International gave the reasons for its conclusion that the government's information did not invalidate any of the organization's findings.

Most arrests are made by police officers, often in plain clothes and using cars without number plates. Arrests and interrogations are also carried out by paramilitary forces stationed in Punjab: the BSF, mainly operating in the districts bordering Pakistan, and the CRPF. Since May 1990 all security forces in Punjab have operated jointly under the command of the state's director general of police.

INDIA

In late 1991 the whole of Punjab was designated a "disturbed" area, giving the army extensive powers to act in aid of the civilian forces, including the power to detain people without the approval of the courts.

Torture takes place in official places of detention, notably police stations. Other places where torture is reportedly often used are: Beeco Interrogation Centre, Batala; Ladha Kothi Jail; the CRPF Headquarters at Mal Mandi, Amritsar, and the police stations and headquarters of the Criminal Investigation Agency (CIA). However, some detainees have been tortured in secret detention centres located in private houses. In most cases, torture occurred while detainees were denied access to the outside world and were held in unacknowledged detention.

The most common methods of torture reported include hanging people from the ceiling and beating them or using them as a human swing, forcing their legs wide apart causing pelvic injury, rolling iron or wooden bars across the thighs, beating the genitals and inserting chili powder into the rectum and other sensitive parts of the body. Some torture victims claim they have been given electric shocks.

In a sworn statement given in July 1990 Piara Singh, a 68-year-old man from Rattan village, Ludhiana district, described how his family was harassed by police who were searching for his son, a student activist. Piara Singh said he was severely tortured while in detention: his legs were pulled apart to 180 degrees, a heavy steel roller was rolled on his thighs and he was hung upside down from the ceiling with his hands tied behind his back. He believed that he was tortured because he was unable to give information about his son's whereabouts.

Women and girls in Punjab have also been tortured. The problem became so acute that in 1989 the Governor of Punjab instructed the police not to bring any woman to a police station for questioning: they were only to interrogate women in front of village elders or similar representatives of the community.

Torture also appears to have been used in reprisal for the activities of armed opposition groups. At the end of August 1990 some 200 residents of five villages near Kathunangal were reportedly rounded up and beaten by members of the CRPF, who took some of them to Thiriawal CRPF station and tortured them. The incident occurred the day after a landmine had exploded and damaged a patrol jeep. One of a number of journalists who saw the villagers reported that: "Many of them could not walk and showed injuries on the limbs. Electric shocks were given to some of them".

A local civil liberties group, the Punjab Human Rights Organization, investigated the villagers' allegations and reported details of 18 cases of alleged torture: two young men had their thighs cut and then had powdered red chilies rubbed into the wounds, as well as being tortured with electric shocks. Another had his fingernails torn out and the flesh on his hands cut. Partap Singh had been beaten with leather belts. Two of those tortured were only 12 and nine years old. Most of the villagers were reportedly released the evening after their arrest. A magisterial inquiry reportedly found that some people had been beaten by the CRPF but no action is known to have been taken against the perpetrators.

The use of torture in Punjab has been officially confirmed. A judicial investigation was conducted in February 1989 by Justice S.S. Sodhi, in Amritsar jail. He found that many detainees had been tortured by police when kept in illegal detention preceding formal arrest.

Even when medical reports have confirmed the use of torture there has often been no further action. Surinder Singh was detained by the police on 30 November 1990, and subjected to torture. He was released on 22 December after a *habeas corpus* petition was filed in the High Court of Punjab and Haryana by his father. In a statement to the court on the day of his release Surinder Singh alleged that he had been illegally detained, that no case had been registered against him and that his arrest had not been entered in the daily register. He told the court that he had been tortured and it ordered that he be medically examined. The medical report stated that Surinder Singh was unable to walk and described 18 scars, abrasions and bruises on his body, adding that all these injuries could have been caused by torture and appeared to have been inflicted in the period during which Surinder Singh was in detention. However, the High Court did not recommend any further investigation into the allegations of torture.

Police officers accused of responsibility for torture and other human rights violations have at most been suspended or dismissed from service. In early 1990 the director general of police told a visiting delegation of members of the European Parliament that in the first two months of 1990 seven police officers had been suspended and one dismissed for "crimes against the populace".

2

Deaths in custody

The ultimate form of torture is that which results in the victim's death. There is evidence of a pattern of this form of gross human rights violation throughout India, regardless of which party is in power at the centre or in the states.

The evidence

"...the policemen came into the room ... and started beating Ram Swaroop. They took him out of the room. After a long time the policemen brought back Ram Swaroop who was all covered in mud ... Ram Swaroop kept on writhing in pain and asking for water. Dandwa asked the policemen for water and was told to go to sleep or he would be beaten in the same way as Ram Swaroop. When Dandwa told the policemen that Ram Swaroop was dead the policemen...told us to put clothes on the body of Ram Swaroop. Then one big built policeman put the corpse on his shoulder and said they were taking him to the hospital.... After dawn the policemen returned and told us that ... we [should] not tell anybody that Ram Swaroop is dead."

This is a sworn statement by Pratap, one of 10 migrant men who worked at the Naraina fly-over in New Delhi. On 16 September 1988 they were beaten by police officers from the Inderpuri police station when they requested payment for work the police had compelled them to undertake for less than the statutory minimum wage. Ram Swaroop, aged around 50 and from Azadpur, belonged to the Bawaria tribe. He did not survive the beatings and died the next morning. His body was thrown into a nearby canal. The police said they had interrogated him about criminal activities they sus-

CHAPTER 2

pected his sister to have committed. Press reports later suggested that one of the police officers had confessed to having dumped the body in a canal and had said he did so on the orders of the station house officer.

This case is rare not only because it gives a first-hand account of the torture of a man who died in police custody, but also because the police acknowledged the crime. In an affidavit sworn on 3 January 1989 Deputy Commissioner of Police, A.S. Khan, admitted that Ram Swaroop had died because of police beatings. Commissioner Khan had served previously under Vijay Karan, one of the few police commissioners in India to have publicly declared that he would work hard to eradicate torture.

In Bombay Raju Mohite, a *dalit*, died in Bhagwati hospital on 6 July 1990 the day after he had told his family, on his release from Oshiwara police station, that he had been tortured. According to his relatives, they and a lawyer had been refused permission to see him after his arrest on 26 June in connection with a burglary. On 5 July Raju Mohite was brought before a magistrate and released. He was able to get home only with the help of a lawyer because of injuries he had sustained. His eldest brother, Balu, was reported to have said that Raju Mohite's "toes had been smashed, his legs were swollen and the entire lower part of his body as well as his back had turned green and black. With great difficulty he spoke to us and told us that the police had repeatedly beaten him to make him confess to an offence". They took Raju Mohite to hospital immediately but he died the next day. The police said he had suffered from jaundice and that his injuries had been caused by a "fall" or "accident". This, however, was contradicted by a post-mortem examination which found 19 injuries on his body apparently inflicted with a "hard and blunt object". These injuries, which were consistent with the dead man's torture allegations, were said to have been inflicted during the last four days of his life, three of which he had spent in police custody.

There is overwhelming evidence that widespread torture often leads directly to deaths in custody. Such evidence has emerged from government officials and official institutions, the courts, doctors who have carried out post-mortem examinations on prisoners who have died in custody, and the police themselves. In January 1985 the then Chief Justice of India's Supreme Court noted that only rarely was eye-witnesses' testimony of torture leading to death available, other than from police officers who tend to be more

INDIA

concerned to conceal than to acknowledge what has occurred. The Chief Justice made this observation after the Allahabad High Court had acquitted certain police officers of torturing to death a suspect in Uttar Pradesh on the grounds that there was insufficient evidence to prove the case beyond reasonable doubt. Prompted by the Allahabad High Court's decision, the Supreme Court proposed amending the Evidence Act to ensure that police officers who commit human rights violations against people in their custody should not evade punishment due to a "paucity of evidence". The Supreme Court said that it wished to "impress upon the government the need to amend the law ... so that the burden of proof in cases of custodial death will be shifted to the police"[24]. Shortly afterwards, in June 1985, the Law Commission of India proposed that the Evidence Act should be amended, by creating a new Section 114 B, to provide a rebuttable presumption that injuries sustained by a person in police custody had been caused by the police officer in charge of his custody. Successive Indian governments, however, have failed to implement this recommendation.

Official police bodies have also condemned torture. Following the 1975 — 1977 emergency, which saw widespread excesses, a National Police Commission (NPC) was established in 1979 to inquire "into the system of investigation and prosecution ... the use of improper methods, and the extent of their prevalence". After one year of work, the NPC reported, while condemning torture in the strongest terms, that:

> "... Nothing is so dehumanising as the conduct of police in practising torture of any kind on a person in their custody. Police image in the estimate of the public has badly suffered by the prevalence of this practice in varying degrees over several years. We note with concern the inclination of even some of the supervisory ranks to countenance this practice in a bid to achieve quick results by short-cut methods."[25]

The police at state level have acknowledged the use of torture. For example, following a rising number of deaths in police stations in Andhra Pradesh during 1985 and 1986, the Andhra Pradesh Police Association openly urged police officers to cease using torture and adopt instead "modern scientific methods of investigation". In Delhi, Police Commissioner Vijay Karan told the press on his appointment on 1 May 1988 that he "would like to ban torture

CHAPTER 2

and third degree methods". He maintained that "the police have no right to beat up anybody". During his tenure as police commissioner, the use of torture during interrogation was banned in Delhi police stations. In January 1989 Commissioner Karan established a Central Checking Team of Vigilance Staff whose task it was to visit police stations without warning to ensure that prisoners' rights were not being violated. This appears to have had a significant effect: in 1989 and 1990 the number of deaths in custody in Delhi police stations fell by a half compared to previous years. In fact, torture did not cease in Delhi's police stations and other factors may have contributed to the reduction in custodial deaths, but according to one commentator, in March 1990: "Mr Vijay Karan's recent annual report has shown that the practice of third degree was effectively contained for the whole of last year without any adverse impact on the role and functioning of policing in Delhi"[26]. It may also be noteworthy that the number of people who died in police custody in Delhi rose considerably in 1991, after Vijay Karan's term as police commissioner ended.

In August 1991 the Minister of State for Home Affairs, M.M. Jacob, told the Lok Sabha, India's lower house of parliament, in response to the increase in custodial deaths in Delhi, that he was "determined to take deterrent action against those exceeding or abusing their powers". He said that an inquest was being held into the death of Jairam Singh, a 50-year- old man who died in police custody on 19 August and that three police officers had been charged with murder. K.K. Birla, a member of the Rajya Sabha, India's upper house of parliament, described Jairam Singh's death as an example of the "ruthless style in which the police deals with the suspects and contravenes the provisions of law". He reportedly urged the government to take note of the growing number of deaths in police custody in the country and to remove "outdated and brutal methods" to conduct investigations and interrogations.

Officials and members of the legislative assemblies in Maharashtra, West Bengal, Andhra Pradesh and other Indian states have also spoken out against torture. In mid-1990 a heated debate took place in the Maharashtra state assembly after allegations that three people had been beaten to death by the Maharashtra police in the space of three weeks. The minister of state for home affairs announced that a new code of conduct for the police, outlining arrest and detention procedures, had been prepared. This apparently included a requirement that all detainees should be given a medical examination immediately after arrest and stipulated that the police should keep diaries to record all transfers of detainees. Curiously, however, little is known of this new code, or its implementation, although it was announced as long ago as July 1990. Two weeks afterwards, senior police officials were apparently unaware of its existence. A year or so later members of the state legislative assembly were again condemning the "third degree" methods used by the police to extract "confessions" after Sheikh Jam Zakir, a 16-year-old boy, had been tortured to death at the Jensi Nagar police station in Aurangabad. On that occasion members of the state assembly called for drastic changes in the training of police personnel and for the punishment of the police concerned.

During the 1977 state elections in West Bengal, the Left Front government pledged to inquire into the many cases of custodial deaths and political murders committed during the previous seven years of Congress rule in the state. Two commissions of inquiry were formed, but their findings are not known to have been published, nor were police officers brought to justice, as the government had promised. Ten years later, in October 1987, Jyoti Basu, Chief Minister of West Bengal, condemned deaths in police custody in the strongest terms, Calcutta's commissioner of police having announced that "no under trial should die in police custody". Yet reports of custodial deaths have continued. In September 1989 Jyoti Basu said that 71 people had died in police custody in West Bengal between December 1985 and December 1988.

In Andhra Pradesh three deaths, allegedly caused by torture, in one week in September 1986 led the then chief minister to announce that a judicial inquiry had been ordered into every case of death in police custody in the state[27]. He also promised that police officers guilty of such crimes would be punished severely and that measures would be taken to prevent torture. But of the 31 deaths in custody Amnesty International knows of since 1985 it has recorded suspensions of police officers in no more than nine cases, transfers in one case and one in which police were tried or convicted.

Judges in Andhra Pradesh and elsewhere have sometimes pointed to clear police responsibility for directly causing suspects' deaths through torture. In April 1988 the Andhra Pradesh chief minister put before the state legislative assembly the report of a judicial inquiry into the death of a prisoner, T. Muralidharan, in Vijayawada police station in September 1986. He had been found hanged and had seven wounds on his body. The police officers who had custody of him had given contradictory statements about his death, finally claiming that he had committed suicide[28]. However, K. Sriranganayakulu, the judge who conducted the investigation, found evidence of causing his death against four police officers. They concluded that the sub-inspector of Vijawada police station was "directly responsible for the death of T. Muralidharan, having intentionally caused body injuries which were sufficient ... to cause death".

High court judges have also found evidence that police officers had caused deaths in custody even when the police, and initially in one case a state government, had denied responsibility. The case was that of Mohammed Idris, reportedly a well-known criminal, who was arrested on 27 March 1984. He died in custody at Calcutta's Lal Bazar police station the day after his arrest on suspicion of involvement in the killing of a West Bengal deputy police commissioner. On 1 April Chief Minister Jyoti Basu told the state legislative assembly that the death of Mohammed Idris had resulted from a merciless assault by other prisoners, a version of events the police had announced earlier. However, after a public outcry the chief minister ordered Justice S.C. Deb of the Calcutta High Court to conduct a judicial inquiry. His report was eventually published more than five years after Idris' death, in 1989. Justice Deb found: "... brutal injuries were inflicted on Idris at the time of interrogation ... and had resulted in his death which is unnatural and homicidal.... Multiple serious injuries were inflicted on him and all those injuries were fresh, *ante mortem*[29] and homicidal in nature. Idris was deliberately killed by the Calcutta police."[30]

The Supreme Court also has ruled that deaths have occurred because of torture in police stations. Thiru Kathamuthu, aged 24 and a member of the All India Youth Federation and the Communist Party of India (CPI), was arrested in connection with a case of theft in the Union territory of Pondicherry. The day after his arrest in December 1986 he was taken to hospital suffering burn injuries to 94 per cent of his body; he died shortly afterwards. The police claimed he had committed suicide by setting fire to himself, using matches and a kerosene stove. However, the CPI accused the police of beating him and then burning him to hide what they had done. One report suggested that he had been in handcuffs when he was set alight. The dead man's father brought the case before the Supreme Court which, on 7 September 1989, declared: "... we are inclined to agree ... that a *prima facie* case has been made for initiating prosecution. We therefore direct the respondents to institute prosecution against the concerned Station House Officer and Constable of Dhanwantri Nagar Police Station ... on the footing that during police custody, Thiru Kathamuthu died apparently on account of physical assault followed by burning of the body after drenching it with kerosene".

In another case, that of 35-year-old Gopi Ram who died in August 1986, the Supreme Court ruled two years later that: "it was a *prima facie* case of deliberate murder of an innocent illiterate poor citizen of Delhi in police station and investigation was partisan"[31]. Gopi Ram had been stripped and beaten with iron rods in the Patel Nagar police station, but the police claimed that he had died of morphine and alcohol poisoning.

In 1991 the Supreme Court held that the police's negligence had caused the death of Mahesh Mahto. A photograph in the *Times of India* of the unconscious victim roped to the footboard of an autorickshaw had prompted the Supreme Court Legal Aid Committee to initiate legal action for compensation against the state of Bihar. Mahesh Mahto was one of several men beaten unconscious by railway passengers whose property had been looted at Jamalpur, Bihar. The railway police took him to hospital but claimed they had tied him to the autorickshaw because they had no other transport. The deputy superintendent of police admitted before the Supreme Court that if appropriate care had been given Mahesh Mahto's life could have been saved[32].

The findings of post-mortem examinations carried out on victims of custodial deaths sometimes reveal injuries consistent with torture, but often no further action is taken. Detainees taken to hospital by police rarely feel free to report that they have been tortured in the presence of police guards. One Bombay hospital doctor observed: "Normally the history of torture does not come out. Even if it does we haven't been taught to do anything. Torture is seen as official".

Post-mortem examinations have provided crucial evidence of police responsibility in a number of cases of death in custody. One, in July 1991, was that of a man named Kuttappam who died shortly after being released from Parassala police station in Kerala. A subsequent post-mortem indicated that his spleen had been ruptured by torture in police custody. A 20-year-old labourer named Paramasivam was said to have died of "natural causes" in the

CHAPTER 2

custody of Tamil Nadu police. However, a post-mortem found that he had died of shock due to "vagal inhibition[33] following injuries to his testicles on both sides", suggesting that he too had been tortured.

Despite pressure within the police to condone human rights violations committed by some police officers, several police investigations have confirmed torture. For example, the Corps of Detectives conducted a preliminary investigation into the death of a man in Gulbarga town in the southern state of Kerala in December 1989, and concluded that the victim had been tortured to death. In Andhra Pradesh a police superintendent produced evidence that three of his colleagues had tortured a disabled beggar, Enibeera Peda Venkataiah, who died in custody in April 1988 following his arrest on suspicion of child abduction. His body apparently was mutilated by the police officers responsible for his death in an attempt to prevent its identification.

Numbers

"Deaths in custody are not on the rise", said the Attorney General of India when the United Nations Human Rights Committee asked him about it in March 1991. The Attorney General, appearing during the examination of India's second periodic report under the International Covenant on Civil and Political Rights (ICCPR), did not support his statement with statistical evidence. A few months later, one civil liberties group, the People's Union for Democratic Rights (PUDR), did publish statistics, and these showed an "alarming increase" in Delhi: seven deaths in the first eight months of 1991, already over twice the number for the two previous years. In Andhra Pradesh, *The Telegraph* reported in October 1991, there had "been an increase in the number of 'lock-up deaths' in the state in the last two years of the Congress(I) government". The Supreme Court, in a case decided in August 1988, noted: "... we are gravely concerned at the increasing number of deaths which are reported of persons detained in police lock-ups"[34].

In areas where armed opposition groups are active the figures have risen sharply: at least 26 deaths in custody as a result of torture have been reported in Jammu and Kashmir since the beginning of 1990. During the five month-long "Operation Bajrang" in Assam, at least 12 people died in custody allegedly as a result of torture.

INDIA

Sometimes such deaths occur in quick succession. In September 1991 two custodial deaths were reported in consecutive weeks in Andhra Pradesh; during the last week of June and the first week of July 1990 three deaths were reported in Maharashtra; and in October 1987 there were three deaths in custody within six days in West Bengal.

Amnesty International has received information on 415 deaths in custody allegedly resulting from torture in India since 1985[35]. Since then, Amnesty International has recorded, for example, 61 deaths in custody in Uttar Pradesh, 49 in Bihar, and 43 in West Bengal.

However, these statistics are only a representative sample: the true number of deaths in custody each year as a result of torture is believed to be 100 or more. In June 1988 *The Statesman* newspaper reported that in Tamil Nadu alone as many as 500 detainees had died in custody in the preceding 10 years. In May 1991 the Association for the Protection of Democratic Rights listed 108 deaths in custody as a result of torture which had occurred since the Left Front government came to power in West Bengal in 1977. In Andhra Pradesh at least 104 people died in custody between 1984 and 1988. In July 1986 the *Telegraph* reported that there had been 20 deaths in custody in Uttar Pradesh during the first half of the year. Sources within India have been forced to conclude that custodial deaths are a routine and regular occurrence. *The Sunday Statesman* recognized this in a report which it published in August 1989: the newspaper commented that deaths in custody as a result of torture "seem to take place with sickening regularity in the lesser known police stations all over the country".

Sometimes, cases are reported in local newspapers which it is difficult for civil liberties groups and Amnesty International to obtain. Many others are reported in the local editions of national papers which Amnesty International has been unable to survey on a regular basis.

The poor and the underprivileged, often the victims of torture, have little opportunity to obtain publicity or redress. They are often easy targets for police intimidation. Their torture in custody usually becomes known only if local people make public protests. In July 1986 one newspaper noted that the death in custody of Samir Naksar was reported "only because the local people had actively protested against it. But usually deaths in remote areas are never reported"[36]. Some public protests are violent, as the

CHAPTER 2

Economic and Political Weekly commented in August 1991: "As always, it is only when the law is taken by the people in their own hands that the guardians of the law wake up. Following the death of ... Jairam Singh ... the people of the locality surrounded the police station, blocked the roads, set fire to vehicles and stoned the police. This compelled the police to rush to the spot and suspend three policemen". However, in other cases violent protests provided a pretext for not proceeding against the policemen whose misbehaviour caused the public to protest in the first place.

The victims

A survey carried out by the PUDR, published in August 1991, showed that almost all those who die in custody in Delhi come from economically weaker sections of society. This is a long-standing pattern. "Senior police officials admit that it is only the 'small fry' who usually die in police custody" reported *The Telegraph*, in July 1986. Those most likely to die in custody come from underprivileged groups within Indian society. These include *dalits* and *adivasis*, including women belonging to these communities, and members of religious minorities. Children and the old and infirm are also among the victims. Victims from these groups have often been arrested as suspects in petty criminal cases. Political prisoners and suspected opponents of the government have also died in custody, especially in areas where armed opposition groups are active, including both those seeking independence or increased autonomy and those like the *Naxalites* who call for greater economic and social rights.

Some of those who have died in police custody appear to have been innocent of any crime. Often they were detained illegally with no case or charge registered against them. Once a prisoner's death has occurred it appears to be common for police to implicate the victim in a crime or else deny that they had been detained at all. Other deaths in custody have been reported of people who were being held in place of people, particularly family members, who were wanted by the police. One was Khurshid Ahmed, a 20-year-old *adivasi*, who died in the Punhana police station, Haryana, on 24 August 1991. He was arrested because a relative in debt to a local dairy owner, who had complained to the police, could not be traced. In numerous cases people appear simply to have incurred the displeasure of particular police officers — perhaps by being

INDIA

unable to pay a bribe demanded by the police, or because they threatened to expose police corruption and extortion. Yet others have been victimized by police acting in collusion with powerful interest groups, such as politicians or landlords. In Sikkim state Dharma Dhitta Sharma, a Congress(I) activist and political rival of the chief minister, was reportedly killed in February 1988 after being beaten at Soreong police station. The only known official reaction was the suspension of two policemen from duty.

Jairam Singh, a 50-year-old labourer, died in the custody of Patel Nagar police, Delhi, on 19 August 1991. His death was the seventh reported in Delhi in the first eight months of 1991. It was widely reported in the press and raised in both India's houses of parliament, and was the subject of two official inquiries.

There were no charges against Jairam Singh who, according to some press reports, simply accompanied his 12-year-old son, Manoj, to the police station. Both were detained on 18 August after Manoj allegedly stole a purse. The police said that Manoj confessed voluntarily to the crime, but the family alleged that the police had forced him to confess and that he was, in fact, at the cinema at the time of the theft. The contents of the purse were not recovered and there was press speculation the case could have been falsely registered.

Relatives of the father and son alleged that both were tortured by the police. Jairam Singh was said to have had his hands tied behind his back and to have been beaten mercilessly. When a PUDR team saw Manoj on 21 August 1991 his body was reportedly still swollen from beatings, and *lathi* marks were clearly visible.

Jairam Singh reportedly complained of stomach pains and problems with urinating on 19 August and was taken by police to the Khera nursing home where, after treatment, he was declared to be "in a position to leave". A medical note apparently stated that he had a clear chest and was conscious. However, 10 minutes later he collapsed and died. A post-mortem examination found that his death was due to the cumulative effect of injuries. The PUDR report publicly condemned what it described as the "appalling negligence of the doctors" in a case "if not of blatant collusion at least of fatal callousness".

After news of Jairam Singh's death spread, a crowd gathered in protest outside Patel Nagar police station, attacked vehicles and police officers, and was forcibly dispersed by the police using *lathis* and tear-gas.

CHAPTER 2

After initial inquiries, Delhi Police Commissioner Arun Bhagat acknowledged that "maltreatment" had occurred. Three police officers were suspended and a case of culpable homicide not amounting to murder was registered. After receiving the post-mortem report, however, the charges were changed to murder and wrongful confinement, and the three suspended police officers were arrested. The station house officer of Patel Nagar police station was transferred — a decision criticized by the PUDR as an example of "the failure and lack of will when it comes to disciplining higher officials and making them accountable for what happens in their jurisdiction [which] has perpetuated the dehumanising processes of 'law and order' maintenance in our society".

An inquest into the death was conducted by a magistrate and there were further inquiries by the Delhi police but to date the three police officers who were arrested are not known to have stood trial.

Criminal suspects

The majority of those who die in police custody are people tortured in order to extract a confession or further information about a crime. Many were suspected of criminal offences such as burglary, theft, robbery, arson or public order offences. Others had been detained for trivial reasons such as "moving suspiciously" or travelling on a train without a ticket. Children as young as 14 have been among the victims, as have people who were ill or physically disabled.

Channaiah, a 40-year-old autorickshaw-driver, died in Subramanyanagar police station, Bangalore, on 18 May 1988 after being arrested in connection with a criminal investigation. His wife, Parvati, said he was arrested six days earlier but the police said they had arrested him only on 17 May 1988. They said they had found him hanging by a blanket from the door of his cell and that, although he was still alive when found, their efforts to revive him had failed.

Parvati challenged the police claims of suicide. She said that when she had tried to see her husband on 15 May she had not been allowed to do so. She alleged that the police later told her that Channaiah had complained of stomach ache, implying that it had somehow contributed to his death. She also claimed that they had offered her a bribe and some employment to keep quiet about her suspicions.

Other sources also questioned the police version of events, as Channaiah was reportedly seen by a municipal official at the police station on both 15 and 16 May while held in unacknowledged detention by the police. A magistrate went to Subramanyanagar police station the day of Channaiah's death, saw the body and ordered its transfer to hospital for a post-mortem examination. The following day Channaiah's body was removed from the hospital and cremated, without the family being notified. Three police officers had been suspended on the day of Channaiah's death but it is not known whether they were disciplined or prosecuted.

Minority groups — Muslims
Half of India's Muslims live in three states: Bihar, Uttar Pradesh and West Bengal. Most allegations of police torture, extrajudicial executions and "disappearances" of members of the Muslim community come from Uttar Pradesh, the state with the largest Muslim minority — about 15 per cent of the population. Tension between the Muslim and Hindu communities in Uttar Pradesh has led to communal riots and widespread killing on several occasions, most recently in June 1991. The force responsible for many violations reported against Muslims in Uttar Pradesh is the Provincial Armed Constabulary (PAC), the 32,000-strong riot police drawn almost exclusively from the Hindu majority.

After communal rioting in Meerut in May 1987 during which the official death toll was put at 91, over 600 people were detained in the Hashimpura area of Meerut during search operations carried out by the PAC. According to press reports, 32 of them "disappeared" and were presumed killed. Aged between 13 and 65, they were reportedly taken by truck to the banks of the Upper Ganga canal near Muradnagar by the PAC. Here they are believed to have been shot in secret and their bodies thrown into the canal. Two survivors have testified that they were taken to the canal by uniformed men whom they identified as members of the PAC. However, the PAC have denied responsibility for the killings.

Inquiries were reportedly carried out by the CBI, the CID and a three-member official investigation team headed by former auditor general Gian Prakash. The findings of the official inquiries — the latter reportedly blamed the PAC for the murders — have still not been made public. Nonetheless, the Indian Government has said that *ex-gratia* payments were made to relatives of 13 people whose bodies were found and identified, and to 17 of the other 19 people killed whose bodies had not been found. In making these payments, the government did not accept official responsibility for the killings.

At least a dozen other Muslims were reportedly tortured to death

CHAPTER 2

in May 1987, five in Meerut District Jail and seven in Fatehgarh Central Jail. Four of the deaths in Fatehgarh Central Jail occurred on 25 and 26 May. The victims — Mohammed Hanif, Salim Siddiqui, Deen Mohammed and Mohammed Osman — had been arrested on 22 May. A district magistrate visited the prison to inquire into the deaths but denied allegations that the deceased had been beaten to death by police officers. He cited post-mortem reports as substantiating this, but these were never made public.

According to information received by Amnesty International, the arrested men were repeatedly beaten by police, PAC personnel and, at the instigation of the PAC, by criminal convicts. Deen Mohammed's father reportedly learned of his son's death when he was taken to the jail on 29 May. He was then apparently ordered to bury the body before dawn.

Allegations of torture causing deaths in custody of Muslims persist. For example, in May 1989, Mohammad Mumtaz was arrested by the Barhi police in Bihar in connection with communal riots in Hazaribagh. Police claimed that he jumped from a jeep into the Barakar river and was fatally injured. However, his family said that he had one arm in plaster and was handcuffed which would have prevented an escape attempt, and that he was killed in police custody. The Congress(I) representative for Gaya district stated that the killing of Mohammad Mumtaz in police custody had lowered the party's reputation among the minority Muslim community. A writ petition was filed by relatives of the deceased requesting access to the body for identification and a post-mortem examination. This was granted by the Ranchi bench of the Patna High Court, which ordered the authorities to reveal the place of burial. A magisterial inquiry was ordered. The deputy commissioner and superintendent of police said action would be taken against the guilty policemen after the inquiry, the results of which are not known.

Dalits and *adivasis*

The vulnerability of *dalits* and *adivasis* has led to many deaths in custody as a result of torture and brutality.

Deaths of *dalits* in police custody are particularly common in certain states, Bihar for example. The *Sunday Observer*, in January 1988, stated that 16 *dalits* had died in Sasaram prison in Rohtas district, Bihar, between November 1983 and January 1988, allegedly because of ill-treatment and torture. Four died in the month of June 1987 alone. However, *dalits* die in custody throughout India. One case is typical of the pattern.

INDIA

Sekar, a law student aged 25, died in the context of a wage dispute between landlords and villagers, mainly *dalits*. The police apparently intervened on the side of the landlords at a time when there was already tension between landlords and *dalits* in several villages along the border between Tamil Nadu state and the Union Territory of Pondicherry. Two *dalit* youths, Sekar and Kandan, were reportedly shot by police at Panaiyadikuppam in Pondicherry on 2 September 1989. Kandan is said to have died immediately but Sekar was apparently only injured in the leg: according to his relatives he died later in police custody as a result of beatings.

A First Information Report issued by the local police on the day of the shooting said it had taken place at the village of Sorapur in Tamil Nadu, where police and villagers had been attacked. Kandan and Sekar were said to have been shot when police opened fire to disperse the rioters. The police claimed that Sekar died on the way to hospital from injuries sustained during the firing, but this was disputed by eye-witnesses and in a report produced by the Peoples Rights Protection Movement (PRPM), a local human rights group.

A PRPM fact-finding team obtained information from local people and other evidence which suggested that the shootings had actually taken place in Panaiyadikuppam, Pondicherry, and that the circumstances did not warrant the police action. The PRPM reported that a week after the shootings local state officials asked the parents of the two victims to sign statements suggesting that the deaths of their sons had occurred in Sorapur in return for substantial cash payments and the promise of a job opportunity for one member of each family. However, the parents refused to sign the statement and said that the deaths had taken place in Panaiyadikuppam, not Sorapur.

The Tamil Nadu state government ordered an inquiry into the incident on 9 September 1989. On 4 and 5 October 1989 Kandan's wife and Sekar's mother both submitted sworn affidavits to the inquiry in which they said that the shootings had taken place in Panaiyadikuppam, and that Kandan, Sekar and others had not taken part in the disturbances at Sorapur village.

Sekar's mother said in her statement: "I found the police dragging my son towards the limits of Tamil Nadu.... I ran behind the Tamil Nadu police and beseeched them to leave my wounded son and not to carry him away.... The two policemen went dragging my son by his legs. My son's body was lying on his back and he was bleeding profusely."

CHAPTER 2

    The police then put Kandan's body and Sekar in a police van and drove away. Sekar's mother believed that the police had beaten and killed her son because they feared that the "truth would come out if my son, who has been wounded in the leg remained alive. They have beaten him and killed him". She claimed in her affidavit that witnesses were afraid to appear before the inquiry as they feared reprisals by the Tamil Nadu police. The outcome of the inquiry is not known. A Supreme Court writ petition filed in 1990 by a Madras-based advocate urged that interim compensation be paid to the families of the deceased and injured pending further proceedings and that the police authorities in Tamil Nadu supply copies of post-mortem and inquest reports to their families.

    Women from the *dalit* and *adivasi* communities are also liable to be subjected to brutal custodial violence. Moti Birua, a 25-year-old tribal woman, died in police custody at the Manjhari police station, Singboom District of Bihar, on 13 December 1988. The police had apparently wrongly implicated her in the murder of her boyfriend, Rajendra Saveya alias Raja, and taken her for questioning on 10 December. She was apparently seen being beaten after arrest.

    Two days after her arrest, the police took Moti Birua back to her house and searched it. They found red paint marks which they apparently mistook for blood. Claiming that Rajendra Saveya had been killed in the house, they reportedly abused Moti Birua physically and verbally and threatened her with sexual violence. She was then taken back to the police station and died that night or early the next morning. The police claimed that she had escaped from custody and committed suicide by hanging herself from a tree where they later found her body. Her family and local residents, however, allege that she was gang-raped and tortured to death by the police.

    Forum Against Police Repression, a local organization, investigated into Moti Birua's case. They reported that her mother and brother-in-law had gone to Manjhari to obtain her release only to be told that she had committed suicide and that her body was to be taken to Chaibasa for a post-mortem. They were able to view her body and saw what they believed were marks of torture. Moti Birua's mother cleaned her daughter's body, and said she found signs of rape. They questioned the police about her death and were given contradictory information about where she allegedly hanged herself.

    A post-mortem apparently revealed that Moti Birua had died of abrasion of the intestines and had wound marks above her navel. There were no signs of hanging, however, and the pathologist did not investigate whether she had been raped. The body was apparently buried under police supervision.

The two police officers involved were suspended on the grounds that they had behaved suspiciously and negligently, although neither was arrested. A case of murder was registered against them.

After public pressure from the Communist Party of India, the Jharkhand Mukti Morcha, and the Vidyarthi Parishad (Student's Union), a judicial inquiry was ordered by the Singboom Deputy Commissioner, Sashikant Sharma. After three sittings no witnesses could be found who were willing to give depositions before it. The press reported that there was evidence that the police had threatened the villagers not to cooperate with any investigation. Amnesty International does not know of the inquiry's outcome.

Victims of armed conflict

Victims of death in custody were tortured during interrogation or when held during counter-insurgency operations in areas where armed opposition groups are active. In northeast India, Jammu and Kashmir and Punjab, most human rights violations are attributed to the army, including the Assam Rifles, and paramilitary forces such as the CRPF and BSF. Other victims have included people suspected of involvement in political campaigns for land reform, higher wages, or autonomy for tribal regions.

Dhruvajyoti Gogoi died in army custody in Assam in 1991. He was one of at least 12 people who died in custody in Assam during "Operation Bajrang". Reported to be an ULFA member, he was first arrested under the TADA in 1989 and released on bail. Sometime later the wife of a local superintendent of police was killed in an ambush on the road from Tinsukia to Dibrugarh. The police apparently suspected Dhruvajyoti Gogoi of involvement in the murder.

On 17 March 1991 he was arrested by the army at Doomdooma, Tinsukia. A *habeas corpus* petition was filed at the Guwahati High Court to which the authorities were given a week to respond. But on the night of 19 March, the army handed over his dead body to the police.

The army stated that the cause of death was epilepsy. However, a photograph of the dead man's body indicated that both his arms had been broken, that he had suffered a stab wound, and injuries to his legs and face. The post-mortem report, conducted at the Assam Medical College Hospital, noted that he had a perforated liver and 28 injuries on his body. Despite these findings, strongly suggestive of torture, no inquiry is known to have been held into the cause and circumstances of Dhruvajyoti Gogoi's death and no army personnel are known to have been arrested or prosecuted.

INDIA

Baljit Singh, one of over 30 men and boys who were deliberately blinded with thick needles and acid by the Bihar police between October 1979 and November 1980 in apparent attempts to deter other criminal suspects. The Bihar Government disclaimed responsibility, arguing that its officers had acted ouside the law. Only nine police officers are known to have been convicted for their part in blinding just five prisoners. (see pages 10-12)

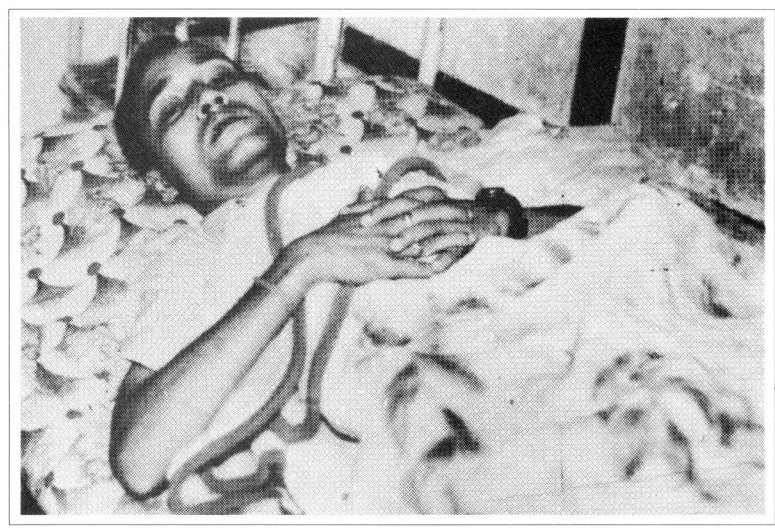

Rajumoni Bezbarooah, a student at Gauhati University, pictured in March 1991 at Golaghat Civil Hospital, Assam, where he was treated after torture with electric shocks during five days' interrogation in the Golaghat army camp. (see page 25)

CHAPTER 2

*Torture victim Ram Kumar pictured in the operating theatre of Jay Prakash hospital, New Delhi, in August 1987. Arrested on 24 August with his friend Mahinder Kumar, he described how they were tortured in Delhi's Vivek Vihar police station by 15 men who "started kicking us in the stomach and groin. They also laid us on our backs and put large rods across our legs ...others stood on the rods and rolled them back and forth". Both youths were then apparently hung upside down from a rod and beaten with sticks until "Mahinder started vomitting blood". Ram Kumar survived. His friend, whose body was said to have been soaked in blood, died the next day. The "roller" torture described by Ram Kumar has been frequently reported by former detainees.
(see pages 7, 17)*

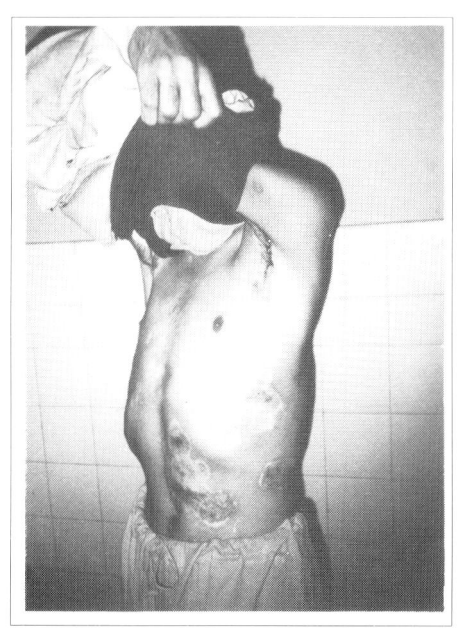

The body of this 25-year-old man from Sopore, Jammu and Kashmir, shows burn marks allegedly made by candles and hot irons during his interrogation by the Border Security Force in Batargam camp, Kupwara, in August/September 1990. He required extensive hospital treatment and has lost the use of his left arm. His name is being withheld for fear of reprisals against him. Torture of political suspects is reported to be routine in army camps and other places of interrogation in Jammu and Kashmir. (see pages 20-24)

51

INDIA

Gross negligence caused the death of Mahesh Mato. The Railway Police at Jamalpur, Bihar, took him to hospital tied to the footboard of a rickshaw after he had been attacked by passengers at the railway station. He died in hospital.(see page 38)

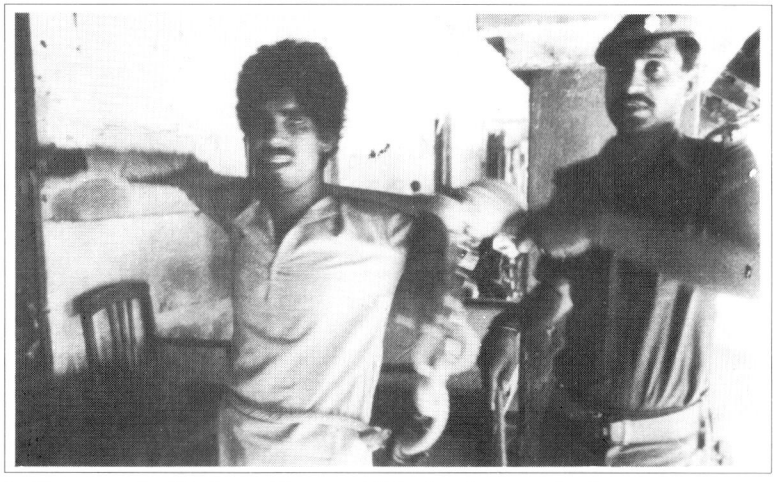

In May 1991 the Hindustan Times published a photograph of a man apparently being tortured in a police station. The caption read: "...Here is Kailash Rai, a suspect, being given the 'aeroplane' by a policeman in Baktiarpur police station... Kailash bowed before the 'aeroplane' and is reported to have confessed to his being a mercenary hired for booth-capturing [stealing ballot boxes] in the forthcoming elections in Bihar." (see page 7)

CHAPTER 2

Banapati Debbarma, a tribal woman raped by soldiers in Tripura. Tribal women in northeast India are often the victims of human rights violations by the army. In March 1991, recognizing this problem, the Guwahati High Court instructed the army not to detain or interrogate women in their camps. (see page 83)

Twelve-year-old Sabina Yasmeen, from Rampur village, West Bengal, was one of several people arrested in February 1990, apparently because their village leader was opposed to the ruling party in the state. She stated: "Four policemen pulled me by my hair while another one hit me with a lathi...one of them tried to urinate in my mouth." (see page 13)

INDIA

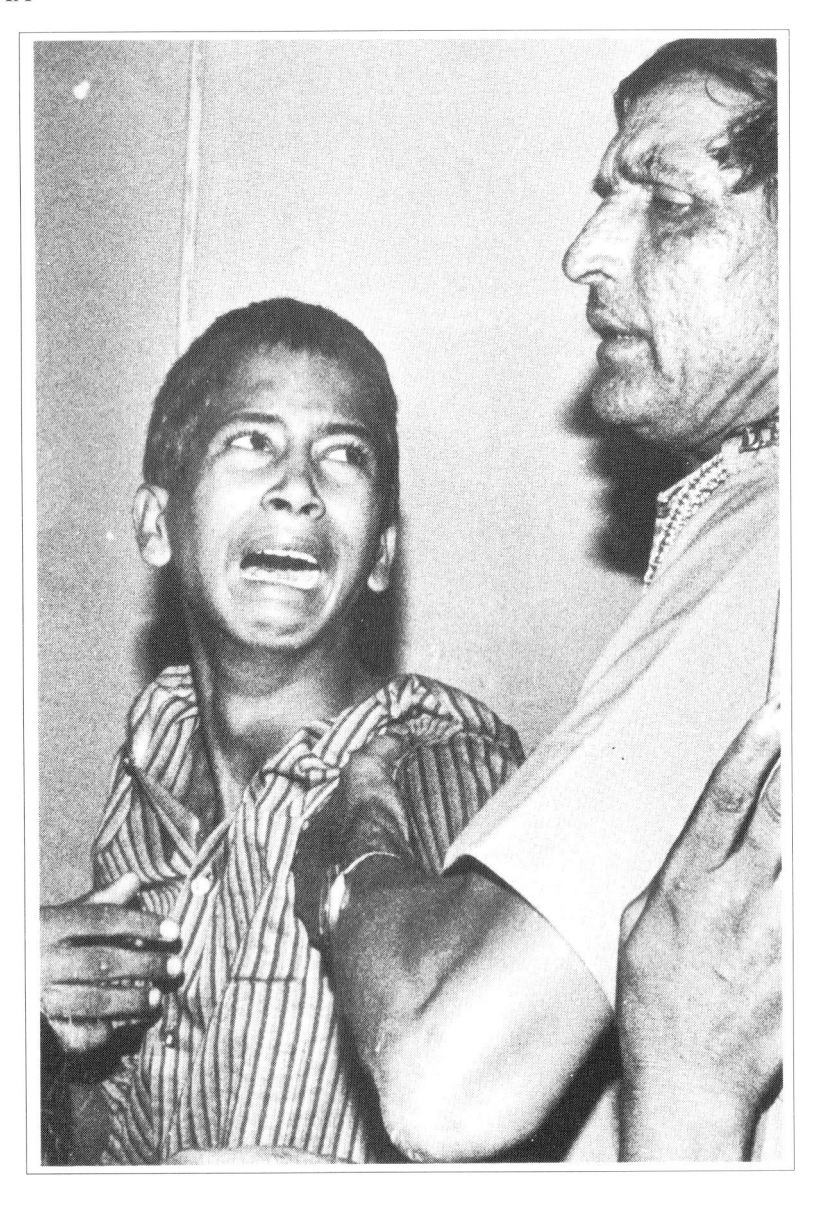

Torture victim Manoj Singh, aged 12, seen after arrest on suspicion of stealing a purse in Delhi in August 1991. His father, Jairam Singh, went with him to a Delhi police station for the boy's interrogation. Jairam Singh is alleged to have been tied up and mercilessly beaten by police - he died hours after his release. A civil liberties team that examined Manoj after he was freed said his body was swollen and bore marks of severe beating. (see pages 42, 43)

3

Impunity: Condoning Custodial Violence

Failure to convict

Successive Indian governments have consistently failed to ensure that proper investigations — a prerequisite for bringing the perpetrators to justice or obtaining compensation for the victims — are held in cases of custodial violence. Indeed, as the Indian press has frequently observed, investigations often appear to be intended more as a response to public pressure than as a systematic means of addressing and preventing human rights violations. The result is that very few police are ever brought to justice for torture.

> "Article 21 of the Constitution lays down that nobody may be deprived of his life or liberty except by a process established by law. Sections 330 and 331 of the Indian Penal Code say that torture of an individual to extract information is a crime punishable with up to 10 years of imprisonment. Death due to torture is murder as defined in Sections 302 IPC for which the maximum punishment is death. Therefore the only lawful course for the Government in the event of death in police custody is to arrest the official concerned and to prosecute him under the above sections. This has not been done in any instance in the country. Normally, a police officer is merely transferred or suspended."[37]

> "...the Government has done pretty little to arraign the guilty. Its reaction depends on the reaction of the people and the press. If the death has not attracted much attention, it is ignored. If it has drawn the attention of the Opposition and the press, a magisterial inquiry is ordered. If the death provokes public reaction in a big

INDIA

> *way, a judicial inquiry is ordered. And yet, no inquiry makes any difference to the victim's family. Nor does it restrain the police from repeating the act.*[38]"

International human rights standards[39], require that governments undertake full investigations into all reports of torture and deaths in custody and bring those responsible to justice. Failure to do so means that the victims and their relatives are denied justice and that the truth is withheld from society at large. Most importantly, the failure to identify and bring those responsible to justice sends a clear message to the perpetrators that their actions are condoned and may effectively encourage them to commit further torture. In India, there is a substantive body of evidence that governments and official agencies have made special efforts to cover-up human rights violations and prevent the police and security forces from being punished.

Amnesty International knows of only three out of 415 cases of custodial deaths which occurred since 1985 in which police officers accused of torturing people to death have been convicted by the courts. The only states in which this is known to have happened are Andhra Pradesh[40], Karnataka (one out of six cases), and Orissa (one out of six cases). In August 1988 two police officers were sentenced to five and eight years' imprisonment on charges of culpable homicide not amounting to murder for assault causing the death in detention of Kashinath Nayak on 3 May 1985 in Orissa. In November 1990, after protracted legal proceedings, seven police officials were sentenced to various terms of imprisonment, including two life sentences, for murdering lawyer M. A. Rasheed, whose body was found two days after he had been taken away by Karnataka police officers. The state's home minister at the time, who had subsequently resigned over the incident and who was accused of instigating his murder, was acquitted. The most recent case known to Amnesty International resulted in a Gujarat High Court judgment on 23 October 1991; six police officers were sentenced to six years' imprisonment for beating Kantuji Mohansinh to death in 1982 and destroying the evidence of their offence. The same police officers had previously been acquitted in May 1983 but, in the only such case known to Amnesty International, the state appealed against that judgment to the court which set aside the acquittal and convicted the police officers.

Police officers have been prosecuted in cases in other states but, to Amnesty International's knowledge, none of these cases resulted in convictions. In Manipur, Rajasthan and Jammu and Kashmir no prosecutions or convictions whatsoever are known to have occurred. Amnesty International's data may be incomplete because not all prosecutions are necessarily reported. However, a study by the PUDR published in August 1991 in New Delhi found evidence of a similar pattern: only nine out of 58 cases of death in custody in Delhi between 1980 and 1991 had resulted in criminal prosecutions. The PUDR concluded that a lack of "demonstrative follow-up action against the erring policemen" was the primary reason for the rise in custodial deaths.

The very few prosecutions that have occurred have almost invariably been the result of years of determined struggle by relatives of the victims seeking justice, rather than official initiatives to enforce the law. Only rarely have relatives succeeded in initiating criminal prosecutions of police officers allegedly responsible for torture[41].

Amnesty International believes that it is often direct or indirect pressure from the executive arm of government which prevents prosecutions. In Uttar Pradesh impunity was effectively granted to members of the Provincial Armed Constabulary (PAC) and prison officials who had allegedly tortured and killed Muslims in their custody during communal rioting in Meerut in May 1987. Hundreds of Muslims were seen being taken away by the PAC; dozens never returned. They are believed to have been secretly killed and their bodies thrown into nearby canals[42].

Two judicial investigations were instituted by the Uttar Pradesh state government: one by Justice Srivastava; the other by former auditor general Gian Prakash. But the inquiry reports were never published. The state government refused to table them in the legislative assembly. According to one authoritative source, the Prakash report "confirmed that 40-60 youths were indeed taken from Hashimpura in PAC trucks and were since untraceable". One resident commented: "So many of our young men were killed...We know the killers, we see them every day. Even the authorities know them. But nothing has been done and nothing will be"[43].

Some of those arrested by the PAC were taken to prison. Seven of them died in Fatehgarh jail of injuries received in police stations and the jail. A magisterial inquiry was held as a result of which two jail guards and two convict warders were suspended. Departmental proceedings were instituted against three prison officials and three cases of murder were registered. However, no prosecutions were initiated.

INDIA

Suspension is the usual official response in the face of a public outcry when someone is killed in custody. In 70 of the cases of death in custody listed in this report, 146 police officers and other officials allegedly responsible were suspended. In many of these cases, suspension appears to have been simply a delaying tactic, until public pressure had subsided or the resources of the victims and their relatives had been exhausted. In August 1989, when seven police were finally suspended five years after Mohammed Idris had been tortured to death in Calcutta's Lal Bazar police station, *The Statesman* commented:

> "What is ... unfortunate is that it took such a prolonged inquiry to identify the culprits, thereby suggesting that there was an attempt at suppression. And while an ordinary citizen would have faced a long prison term, if not the gallows, for such a crime, all that the police authorities have done so far is to 'suspend' the guilty. What incidents such as these demonstrate is not only the double standards that are followed in the application of the law, but also the viciousness that has become an integral part of the police system."

Police officers suspended in connection with deaths in custody have sometimes been promoted shortly afterwards. The director general of police in Calcutta told the press on 11 August 1989 that the officer-in charge of the anti-burglary section, suspended the day before in connection with the death of Mohammed Idris, would be promoted as assistant commissioner if acquitted. After the death of navy seaman T. Muralidharan a number of police officers were suspended, but all were subsequently reinstated and two of them were promoted. In early 1991 a police officer wanted for questioning in connection with the gang-rape of a tribal woman in Orissa was promoted on the express orders of the state police headquarters. Following the torture and death in police custody of Dwarika Thakur in September 1991 in Jehanabad district, Bihar, and the suspension of the two officers allegedly responsible, a press report commented:

> "But as numerous such cases in the past have shown, suspension is no way to punish police officials. In Bihar police officials are suspended one day to pacify the anger of the people against police excesses, and the suspension is revoked the next day. Very often, the

officials, after getting their suspensions revoked, get a 'reward' posting. Indeed in Bihar the number of times a policeman has been suspended, particularly on charges of torturing arrested persons, is taken as a symbol of his professional prowess".[44]

Even if judicial inquiries identify the alleged culprits, state governments frequently fail to prosecute them. In October 1988 the *Deccan Herald*, a Bangalore newspaper, pointed to several cases in which the Andhra Pradesh state government had failed to take: "any action against men in uniform even when they have been held responsible for killing". The newspaper reminded its readers that three separate judicial inquiries into recent deaths in detention had concluded that police officers were directly responsible and had named the officers responsible for what in one case had been described as a "cold-blooded murder". Despite the evidence produced by these inquiries the state government of Andhra Pradesh had initiated no action to punish the culprits: "This is not the first time cops have been found guilty of excesses. Yet, apart from nominal suspensions and perhaps a transfer or two, the culprits in uniform get away scot-free, despite promises by the Government to prosecute them".

There is compelling evidence that the police and other security forces feel free to act with impunity in violating the rights of those in their custody. In parts of the country in which armed opposition are active, immunity from prosecution is explicitly sanctioned by specific legislation. Elsewhere, members of the police and security forces are able to act with impunity because of an informal but nevertheless pervasive and well established system of official complicity in covering up human rights violations.

Legally sanctioned impunity

Special laws in force in states where there is armed insurgency explicitly grant immunity from prosecution to the police and other security force personnel. The Armed Forces (Special Powers) Act, currently in force in Punjab, Jammu and Kashmir, and Assam and other northeast states, gives the security forces wide powers to make arrests, conduct searches without warrant, and to shoot to kill. Section 4 of the act states: "Any commissioned officer, non-commissioned officer or any other person of equivalent rank in the armed forces may ... fire upon or otherwise use force, even to the causing of death, against any person who is acting in contravention of any law or order for the time being in force in the disturbed area prohibiting the assembly of five or more persons or the carrying of weapons or of things capable of being used as weapons..."

In exercising the powers provided in the act, the security forces are granted immunity in advance from possible prosecution. Ordinary legal safeguards do not apply. Section 6 of the act reads: "No prosecution, suit or other legal proceeding shall be instituted, except with the previous sanction of the Central Government, against any person in respect of anything done or purported to be done in the exercise of the powers conferred by this Act".

When the provisions of this act were scrutinized recently by the UN Human Rights Committee, established to monitor governments' adherence to the ICCPR, one member of the Committee drew particular attention to the manner in which such laws can facilitate human rights violations: "In this section which gives immunity both from prosecution and from civil process I find a very dangerous word ... *Purported* is the dangerous thing because anyone killing anybody can say 'Well I thought I was performing my functions"[45].

Amnesty International believes that these provisions of the Act have been interpreted by the security forces as a licence to torture and kill with impunity.

Ordinarily, torture is a crime under Indian law: Sections 330 and 331 of the Indian Penal Code (IPC) provide imprisonment for up to 10 years for anyone convicted of causing hurt to extort a confession or information about an offence. Section 302 makes murder liable to life imprisonment or death. Section 29 of the Police Act, 1861, makes a police officer who commits "any unwarrantable personal violence to any person in his custody" liable to loss of pay for three months or imprisonment not exceeding three months.

Public servants, however, including police and executive magistrates, enjoy considerable protection from prosecution: Section 197 of the Code of Criminal Procedure provides that they can not be prosecuted without prior permission from the government — either state or central government — which employs them. That protection was further strengthened with parliament's adoption of the Code of Criminal Procedure (Amendment) Bill in September 1991. This protects all government officers from any prosecutions for actions taken in the course of duty when a state is under direct rule from the central government. In those states, officials may be prosecuted only with the central government's permission.

Non-legal systems of impunity: systematic cover-up

Several well-established procedural techniques for evading prosecution for human rights violations provide informal but effective impunity for police and security forces throughout the country. These include the systematic cover-up of human rights violations by the police, the security forces, and the government. These techniques are supported by institutional practices and official policies which provide minimal sanctions against those few police or soldiers who are held accountable for custodial violence.

The police regularly resort to a range of techniques to cover-up instances of custodial violence: failure to register complaints, acknowledge detention or to apply other legal safeguards; denial of responsibility; falsification of judicial records and post-mortem reports sometimes by having them carried out at police hospitals; intimidation of witnesses and complainants; and influencing police inquiries by having them conducted by police from the same branch and delaying their outcome and prosecutions. It is not only the police who use these methods; they can often rely on the active complicity of medical doctors, executive magistrates and other officials who contribute to cover-ups by writing false reports or suppressing evidence of police torture. Police cover-ups are so common and frequent an occurrence that police officers have themselves acknowledged their existence: "Everybody knows that the police have their own methods to maintain law and order but you surely don't expect anybody to admit to this officially", one police officer was quoted as telling a *Sunday Daily* reporter in late 1987.

Failure to comply with legal requirements
Chapter 5 of the Code of Criminal Procedure (CCP) lays down the rules the police have to follow when arresting and detaining people. These include informing detainees of the nature of their offence, the grounds for their arrest, and their entitlement to bail[46]. The police are also obliged to produce detainees before a magistrate within 24 hours of arrest[47]. All arrests have to be reported by the officer in charge of the police station to the district magistrate[48]. Non-compliance with these and other provisions for arrest and detention specified in law carry penalties of up to seven years' imprisonment[49]. The police are obliged to register in writing and

keep on record all information relating to the commission of an offence[50].

In some cases, the police have sought to evade responsibility for deaths in their custody by denying that the victims had been arrested or by refusing to register a complaint. This was acknowledged by the *Hindustan Times* in a February 1991 editorial: "Many cases of atrocities still go unreported because of fear of reprisals from perpetrators of the crimes and refusal of the police to register such complaints".

There is no way of knowing how many victims of human rights violations or their relatives have been frustrated in their attempts to bring their complaints before the authorities and to seek redress, but the evidence suggests that they are many.

Indeed, the National Police Commission (NPC) acknowledged the "malady of non-registration of complaints when crimes are reported at police stations", which it recognized as particularly prevalent when complaints related to misconduct by the police, and especially when those complaints were made by the poor. "We are aware that a considerable number who are aggrieved on account of police inactivity or indifference belong to the weaker sections of society who do not have enough resources to pursue their complaints in higher quarters". The commission noted what it considered to be a tendency on the part of the police to suppress information about alleged misconduct, adding that this became "marked" when the misconduct was said to have occurred during the discharge of their duties by the police. The commission added "Examples are: allegations of torture when a person is being interrogated by police during investigation..."[51].

The death of Narasimha Raju, a 20-year-old youth, in the Tilak Park police station in Tumkur, Karnataka, is one example of an attempted police cover-up which came unstuck. According to eye-witnesses, he was taken away by two police officers on 8 July 1990. The same evening a neighbour went to the police station and saw Narasimha Raju there. The young man appeared unwell; the neighbour was told by the police not to come again. The police had told Narasimha Raju's relatives that he would be released after signing some papers in connection with a theft, but three days later he had still not appeared. They then went to the police station to inquire about him, only to be told by a police sub-inspector that he had never been there. They applied to court the next day, arguing that he had been arrested illegally, and again encountered a police denial.

The truth as to what had occurred emerged only when Mutta, a criminal suspect who was detained at Tilak Park police station at the same time, came forward. He stated that on 11 July Narasimha Raju had been taken to the police station's "crime room" and severely beaten by the police, and had died the next morning. He said that he personally had helped load Narasimha Raju's body into a police van, assisted by the van driver. The body was eventually discovered no less than 200 kilometres away, in Chikmagalur. A post-mortem examination noted several injuries on the body. Three police officers were subsequently charged with the illegal arrest, torture and murder of Narasimha Raju, and with destroying evidence. Amnesty International does not know whether they were brought to trial.

Sometimes, the police deliberately fail to record the arrest of persons detained for interrogation, although it is required by law. One such case occurred in West Bengal in October 1987 when two brothers were arrested. One of them, Manohar Jaiswal, died the following day, 24 October. The police said he was the victim of an assault by unknown miscreants, but his brother maintained he had been hung upside down and beaten with *lathis* by a constable and a sub-inspector of police. A subsequent inquiry by the deputy commissioner revealed that the two brothers had been arrested on 23 October, but that their names were not registered in the general diary or in the "lock-up register". It found also that Manohar Jaiswal had been "assaulted severely" inside the police station. Five police officers were suspended as a result for "not maintaining any record of the youth's arrest and for being "morally responsible" for his death, but they are not known to have been prosecuted.

The police also frequently fail to bring detainees before a magistrate within 24 hours of arrest, as the law requires. One reason, clearly, is that this may expose the fact that a suspect has been tortured or ill-treated. In January 1990 Vijay Karan, then commissioner of the Delhi police, made an unannounced visit to Shriniwaspuri police station in South Delhi where at least one death as a result of police torture is believed to have occurred[52]. His visit resulted in the release of nine men who were able to complain to the commissioner that they had been held for several days in connection with a murder investigation but had not been brought before a magistrate within 24 hours of arrest.

The NPC also pointed to police distorting the facts in First

INDIA

Information Reports (FIR). These are used to record the first complaint about an offence and, unlike statements recorded by the police during investigation, can be admitted in evidence during legal proceedings. The NPC commented: "The evidentiary importance attached to the First Information Report...has led to the malpractice of police officers delaying the recording of [a] First Information Report in its natural form and compiling it in a made up manner after taking advice from persons with experience in procedural law"[53].

Several recent cases illustrate the sort of malpractice that has occurred. In one, the report of a the deputy superintendent of the Bombay police into the death in detention of a farmer, Ramu Aba Bhandirge, in November 1989, was described by two high court judges as "not only irregular but illegal". They noted that the FIR had not been filed and that the police inquiry — which had absolved the police by concluding that Ramu Aba Bhandirge had died a natural death — had taken on an "illegal colour". In fact, there were allegations that he had been beaten to death by the police. In another case, involving a similarly suspicious death in custody[54], an Andhra Pradesh High Court judge found that the "records of the police station had been tampered with and superior officers were kept in the dark about the lock-up death".

In West Bengal, the death of a 50-year-old robbery suspect, Matiar Rahman Gazi, in May 1989 was first said by the police to have resulted from his trying to "escape from a moving van". Another person arrested with him, however, refuted this and said that the dead man had been severely tortured after his arrest by being hanged upside down and beaten. A judicial magistrate who examined the case found that the police had tampered with the records: the initial police version attributing the death to an attempt to jump from a speeding police jeep had been "scored through and later rewritten" so as to suggest that Matiar Rahman Gazi had died when he had jumped from a terrace in a bid to evade arrest. "It is really shocking, disturbing and unthinkable to note that a portion of a judicial record had been tampered with in such a naked fashion", the magistrate commented. Subsequently, the chief judicial magistrate for the area found that there was a *prima facie* case against the officer in charge of Hasnabad police station, where the death occurred. As in many other such cases, there were fears that the police would intimidate witnesses. The police officer was instructed not to enter the Hasnabad police station area as "he may gain influence over the witnesses, or threaten them and hamper the trial proceedings".

Distortion of cause of death
In a number of cases, the police have attempted to cover up the torture of detainees who died in their custody by providing false information about the circumstances of the deaths and by denying any responsibility for them. Sometimes they have announced that deaths were due to suicide or illness, accidents, assaults by others, or to injuries sustained when the prisoner tried to escape or resist arrest. Some deaths have been attributed to armed "encounters", with the police denying that the victims were in custody at the time of death.

Police accounts have sometimes been contradictory. The death in detention of T. Muralidharan, a navy seaman who was found hanged at Vijayawada police station in Andhra Pradesh in September 1986, was said by the police to have occurred after he had collapsed in front of the police station and was taken to hospital. Subsequently, the police revised this and said that he had hanged himself at the police station while mentally unbalanced, after he had tried to throw himself into a canal. An injury on his wrist was said by the police to have been caused by a "rat-bite". A senior naval officer who investigated the case, however, found seven injuries on his body, and another man who had been held at Vijayawada police station said he had seen the seaman being brought into the police station and had heard "sounds of torture". This informant also claimed to have heard a voice say, "he is finished", and to have seen the dead man's body being put into a police jeep. A judicial inquiry later concluded that T. Muralidharan's death had resulted from police torture.

Deaths in custody are often attributed to suicide by the police. Chatragadda Sambaiah's death occurred in August 1988 at Eluru police station, Andhra Pradesh. He had been arrested for possessing stolen property. The police said he had hanged himself with a string that he wore around his waist as a belt. His wife alleged that police gave her Rs 2,000 and sent her family to her parents' village after threatening retaliation if she disclosed the circumstances of the death. According to a report in the *Deccan Herald*, in October 1988, the string used as a belt is normally silk or cotton, (and not strong enough to hang a grown man), but that which the police exhibited was a thick nylon rope.

Officials have also frequently claimed that particular deaths in custody were the results of illnesses such as epilepsy, tuberculosis or heart failure, even when the victims were young and apparently healthy. Although some deaths undoubtedly do result from natural causes it is also true that many have been wrongly attributed to natural causes in an attempt to conceal torture. Prakash Ramchandra Kamble, 22 years old and unemployed, died in the custody of Naupada police, Thane, in Maharashtra on 11 November 1987. He had been arrested on suspicion of stabbing someone. The police said he died of heart failure, but this was challenged by a friend who had been arrested at the same time. He said that Prakash Kamble had been brutally tortured by being forced to lie down on a table, with his hands and feet handcuffed, and beaten with a leather belt and iron rods in an attempt to make him confess.

An inquest conducted by the Thane executive magistrate reportedly found that the rear left part of the young man's skull had caved in. Both his ears were blackened with bruises, and one was swollen; his back and shoulders were bruised, blood had congealed on a wound on his left leg; his genitals were bruised, the skin on his right knee had peeled off and his left thigh was swollen. These injuries were believed to have been caused by a belt or sharp instrument. The post-mortem examination found that his death was due to shock caused by multiple injuries. In January 1988 hundreds of people marched to the Thane police station demanding that his killers be brought to justice. However, no action is known to have been taken.

In this case, as in many others the evidence of doctors has been important in challenging police assertions that detainees died due to illness. When Vemula Venkatesh, a factory worker, died in custody in Andhra Pradesh in October 1988, the police said death was due to tuberculosis. But relatives of the dead man alleged that he had been tortured and a post-mortem examination reportedly revealed: "Multiple injuries, burn marks and injuries made by a blunt instrument on the abdomen". According to doctors, there was "no evidence" to support the police claim that he had died of tuberculosis".

In some cases, relatives of deceased prisoners have been put under pressure by the police to sign false statements suggesting that the victims had died from diseases or illnesses from which they had never suffered. Bashir Ahmad died in detention in August 1991 after he was arrested by the police in Andhra Pradesh in connection with a theft. The police said he had died during a fit of epilepsy, but the APCLC, a state civil liberties group, learned that Bashir Ahmad's mother had apparently agreed to sign a statement prepared by the police, stating that her son suffered from epilepsy when this was untrue. The dead man's body reportedly bore scars and other injuries on the nose, neck, right shoulder, back, palms, knees and feet. One leg was badly torn. The injuries were probably inflicted by a blunt instrument and were highly suggestive of torture.

Sometimes the police have admitted that prisoners have died from beatings but said these were inflicted by people other than the police, or were administered by police officers acting in self-defence. Mahendra Singh, a 28-year-old man from the Chhoti Basti in Pushkar, Rajasthan, his 22-year-old brother, Kiran, and their 50-year-old father, Banne, died in police custody on 26 June 1988. The police said the three men had attacked police officers when they were searched for drugs and had been lynched by local residents, although no case was registered against those said to have carried out the lynching. Local residents, however, have contested this version and a man who had been held at the police station on the night of 25 June disclosed that the three men had been brought in by police officers who tied their hands and feet and beat them incessantly with *lathis* until they died. The three were taken to Ajmer hospital but were reported to be dead on arrival.

The deputy superintendent of police, Ajmer, who investigated the case found that the local police version had been "fabricated". A case of murder was brought by the criminal intelligence department and orders were given for the arrest of five police officers, who were said by the deputy inspector general of the CID to have been solely responsible for the deaths. A magisterial inquiry was ordered but its outcome is not known. All 18 police officers in Pushkar police station were transferred. Five were arrested and charged with murder, but no trial is known to have taken place.

In states where armed opposition groups are active police, paramilitary forces and the army often allege that political suspects have died while trying to escape or in an armed "encounter". The exact circumstances of death in such cases can be particularly difficult to establish as police officers are the only witnesses. Their descriptions of what occurred are often so identical as to appear rehearsed. "Escaped" prisoners almost never return home nor are their bodies found. In the case of "encounter" deaths, witnesses sometimes have seen the victims being arrested earlier or while they were in custody but the "encounters" in which they are said to have died rarely result in the death of police officers and are invariably witnessed only by the police, raising suspicion that police claim there was an "encounter" in order to cover up deaths in custody resulting from torture or ill-treatment.

In Manipur, during counter-insurgency operations in Oinam, at least 11 and possibly as many as 15 men were deliberately killed by the Assam Rifles in July 1987. The Assam Rifles claimed that the dead were either killed in armed "encounters" between their soldiers and the NSCN or else had been shot while "trying to escape". This was disputed by eye-witnesses, and senior police officers investigating the alleged "encounters" were said to have found that "they were nothing but 'cold blooded' shooting of villagers". The Guwahati High Court also rejected the explanation put forward by the Assam Rifles when it ruled that the families of B. Wa and P. L. Ring, two of those killed, should receive compensation.

In May 1990 another death occurred in the custody of the Assam Rifles. S. Joel, a 17-year-old, was shot while "trying to escape", according to the police report. Two days before his death the boy had been taken by a patrol to the Assam Rifles' headquarters in Somsai, Ukhrul. The following day he was taken to his brother's house, already showing signs of torture which caused him to have difficulty in walking. He was apparently beaten by soldiers in front of his relatives, who feared for his life, and then taken back to the Somsai headquarters and tortured with electric shocks. The next day, 25 May, his dead body was taken to Ukhrul Police Station. The Assam Rifles attributed his death to his attempting to escape, a claim which, in view of his seriously weakened physical condition, appears highly incredible.

Killings of prisoners in Punjab have also been attributed falsely to armed "encounters" or to escape attempts[55].

Intimidation of witnesses

Police often interfere with evidence by intimidating witnesses. Several judicial officials have confirmed this practice. Justice S.C. Deb of the Calcutta High Court, appointed to inquire into the death of Mohammed Idris in the custody of the Calcutta police, reported in relation to that case:

> *"A show of investigation was made by some officers. Many alleged outsiders and policemen and officers were*

tutored to make untrue statements and their tutored statements were recorded ... An untrue report was intentionally made thereafter by the then Assistant Commissioner of Police (G) Enforcement Branch, Calcutta, to mislead our Hon'ble Chief Minister."

A judge investigating the April 1985 death in Andhra Pradesh of Angadi Prabhakara Rao also pointed to this practice: "before ordering a judicial inquiry, the minimum that is expected is the transfer of the concerned police officers so that witnesses may come forward and depose against the police free from fear".

In some cases the police have gone to extraordinary lengths to prevent the truth emerging, including the confiscation and disposal of bodies of alleged torture victims to prevent their exhumation. This occurred in the case of Basudev Ravani, a 55-year-old coal miner in Bihar's Dhanbad district, arrested in July 1989. The police said he died of alcohol poisoning and a post-mortem examination at the Loyabad Central Hospital was apparently conducted under police guard. The police then buried the body at the cemetery at Telipara. Only then were the dead man's family informed of his death. However, the police apparently refused to say what they had done with his body. Consequently, the relatives went to the hospital, where they were told that the police had found an "unidentified" body and heard that it had been buried at the Telipara cemetery. They went there at once to exhume it, suspecting that Basudev Ravani might have been tortured or beaten to death. When they arrived at the cemetery, 10 or 12 police officers from the Loyabad police station also appeared; they apparently abused the relatives, poured kerosene over the exhumed body and set light to it. Subsequently, a magisterial inquiry questioned the police version of the detainee's death and the officer in charge of the Loyabad police station was suspended. It is not known, however, whether any police officers were prosecuted in relation to Basudev Ravani's death.

More recently, the Punjab police tried to frustrate attempts by relatives to obtain a second post-mortem report to establish the cause of death of Manjit Singh, himself a police constable, who had been arrested on 8 August 1991 on suspicion of murder. He was admitted to hospital nine days later and had died there. The police said that he was suffering from dysentery, but he apparently made a dying declaration to hospital doctors that he had been tortured by his former Chandigarh police colleagues. An inquest was ordered and a medical report was made but the contents were not disclosed. However, there was speculation in the press that the post-mortem report had corroborated the torture allegations and noted contusions on the left side of the body, between the knees and groin, above the ankles and on the face.

After the post-mortem examination, Manjit Singh's father said the police had tried to force him to sign a paper, but that he had refused. If he had signed the paper the police would have been able to claim the body for cremation, despite an order issued to them by a judicial magistrate to stay the cremation until 19 August so as to allow the family the opportunity to have a second autopsy conducted by a board of doctors at the Post Graduate Institute.

In several other cases, relatives of victims of custodial deaths have said the police tried to bribe them, offering them money to keep quiet. The father-in-law of Narasimha Rao, for example, reportedly said police officers had visited him and "promised to pay him a large sum of money if he refrained from giving publicity about the death"[56]. A legal aid lawyer investigating the death of Nakul Bagdi in December 1985 in Bihar said "A senior police officer ... came to me and advised me to drop the case. He advised me that since Nakul's brother had been given a job and since money had been raised privately for his father, it would be futile for FLAC [the legal aid committee] to pursue the case". Yet the post-mortem had stated clearly the body showed signs of physical assault[57].

Witnesses and potential witnesses against the police have been subject to intimidation to prevent them testifying in criminal prosecutions of police officers. A lawyer representing Nakul Bagdi's family said that a police officer had told him: "nobody would give any adverse evidence against the police. And true enough, even the two youngsters who were picked up along with Nakul ... did not turn up to give evidence. They were virtually the eye-witnesses".

Once evidence is found against the police, efforts are often made to reduce the severity of the charge. For example, charges of murder — carrying a punishment of life imprisonment or even death — were initially brought against four Delhi police officers alleged to have tortured and killed Gopi Ram in August 1986. The Supreme Court found evidence of murder, but the charge was changed to the lesser one of endangering life or personal safety under Section 336 of the IPC, for which the maximum penalty is three months' imprisonment. According to one judge, charges against police officers are "diluted time and again".

Police inquiries are also often delayed for years as a means of evading punishment, as noted by *Amrita Bazar Patrika*, a Calcutta newspaper in September 1989. "Some of the cases are already three years old, and no one knows when they will end. By that time fresh cases will pile up and people will lose interest in the old cases and the fate of the culprits. The cases may then be wound up and the accused given a clean chit. There are many ways of sabotaging the process of justice, and prolonging police investigation is one of them."

Involvement of magistrates

Amnesty International has found evidence of magistrates ignoring their legal duty to act when detainees claim they have been tortured or appear in court with clear signs of torture. Accounts have also been received of magistrates issuing false reports which support the police version of events in the face of overwhelming evidence to the contrary.

When someone dies in police custody, a magistrate is obliged to hold an inquiry. Such inquiries are normally held by executive magistrates[58], who are officials belonging to the civil service.

When Angadi Prabhakara Rao died in custody of the Chirala town police in Andhra Pradesh in April 1985, a judicial commission found that his death was a case of homicide and not suicide as the police had claimed. The judge found that the executive magistrate, who had held an inquest into his death, was responsible for falsely certifying there were no visible injuries on the body of the victim. Instead, the judge agreed with the report of the medical officer that there were 12 external injuries on his body and that the victim had died from blows on the stomach and the ribs.

On 29 October 1991 the Supreme Court confirmed such practices when it held that there were grounds to prosecute officials of the Department of Revenue Intelligence for causing the death of Ravi Narang, a 50-year-old businessman in their custody. Ravi Narang's widow alleged her husband had been tortured to death and the Supreme Court ordered a district judge to carry out an inquiry. His findings contradicted the inquest report of the executive magistrate which had attributed Ravi Narang's death to various causes including psychological shock, consumption of morphine, a fight with another prisoner and a fall from the stairs. The judge found that these factors did not cause his death, but that it was probably caused by shock "following a cobweb of injuries sustained through beating and torture".

In some cases judicial magistrates — who are judicial officials appointed by the High Courts and are subject only to judicial control — have also played a part in attempts to conceal the truth. They have done so by ignoring clear evidence of torture when detainees were brought before them by the police to authorize their remand in custody. Sometimes they have also ignored their duty[59] to order a medical examination when a detainee alleges torture by the police.

Nineteen members of the Pardhi tribe, arrested on 13 February 1989 at Khopoli, Maharashtra, on suspicion of robbery and theft, had to wait for one month before the police brought them before a magistrate to authorize their continued detention. All detainees complained of torture. First denied the opportunity to appear in person before the magistrate, they finally did so on 13 March after members of a local civil liberties group had intervened on their behalf. Some complained to the magistrate that they had been tortured and been denied food and medical treatment. Not ordering a medical examination, the magistrate directed that the 19 men be brought before another magistrate, at Vasai. He also failed to order a medical examination, or examine the detainees for marks of torture they said were visible on their bodies. The magistrate simply ordered the police to "give medical treatment whenever required". Assisted by two civil liberties groups bringing a public interest petition, their case was finally put before the Bombay High Court, which ordered a medical examination and criticized the magistrate for having "failed to exercise his duty to inquire into the allegations of ill-treatment in custody". In July 1991 the High Court awarded the men money to pursue their complaints in court, but the policemen whom they say tortured them are not known to have been brought to justice.

Medical aspects of official cover-up

> *"Death and rape in police custody are a very frequent occurrence.... Regrettably, the medical profession now also sometimes joins in these cover-ups and with its help, deaths by torture are transformed into suicides or sudden deaths from chronic diseases like t.b etc."*

This was the comment made by *The Telegraph* newspaper in

CHAPTER 3

November 1986 after the Resident Doctor's Association (RDA) of the All India Institute of Medical Sciences (AIIMS) had accused the police of "interfering in the professional freedom of doctors of the AIIMS".

The RDA statement followed the death in custody of 40-year-old Dayal Singh, a private security guard, at Sriniwaspuri police station on 20 September 1986. He had been arrested on 19 September on suspicion of theft and was declared dead on arrival at the AIIMS the following day. The police maintained that he died of tuberculosis and that there were no marks of injuries on his body. They reportedly put pressure on an AIIMS doctor to confirm this in his report of a post-mortem examination; the doctor apparently complied. However, a subsequent medical examination recorded swelling on the dead man's right hand, fractures of his forearm and contusions and abrasions on his left elbow and both legs. It also found that there was a massive accumulation of blood in the scalp tissue and that the brain was swollen. The injuries indicated application of blunt force sufficient to cause death. The case prompted a public interest petition to the Supreme Court, in which it was alleged that autopsies at the AIIMS were conducted irregularly and that the police were manipulating their findings. On 30 January 1989 the Supreme Court directed that all post-mortem examinations held at the AIIMS should be standardized and conducted by medical officers attached to the Department of Forensic Sciences.

Many victims of police violence are eventually taken to hospital. Many doctors in India, as this report shows, have given detailed and honest accounts of the type of injuries — and their causes — inflicted on some of the men and women brought in by the police for treatment or examination. Doctors have sometimes expressed a sense of helplessness, noting that even when signs of torture have been apparent, the victims rarely make complaints while in hospital because the police are always present. Some doctors, however, have been clearly unable to withstand pressure from the police and local officials to provide post-mortems which assist an official conspiracy to conceal the truth.

In India, post-mortem examinations are carried out at the request of the police or the magistrate conducting an inquiry. A study in 1989 by the PUDR found that many post-mortems in Delhi were conducted by police doctors in police hospitals to which the public had no access. Many private doctors are also believed to have assisted police cover-ups of custodial violence, by failing to record injuries, falsifying records or removing the cause of death from autopsy reports. Justice Deb, investigating the death of Mohammed Idris in Calcutta's Lal Bazar police station, found that a doctor at Calcutta's Medical College Hospital had "falsely recorded that Idris had 'old' marks of abrasion on both wrist joints. He thus created false evidence which is not only an offence but is against his professional conduct". After Uppuleti Chandraiah died in police custody on 9 March 1991 in the Husnabad police station — according to the police he committed suicide, according to fellow inmates he was beaten to death — the government of Andhra Pradesh suspended a civil surgeon of Karimnagar for issuing a false post-mortem report to "save the police"[60].

Falsification of medical records also regularly happens in non-fatal cases of torture. A Supreme Court commission investigating allegations that Gunta Behn Ramji, a tribal woman from Gujarat, had been raped by police in January 1986 found sufficient evidence to conclude that four police officers and two doctors could be charged with "having hatched the conspiracy for destroying the evidence and thereby keeping the accused constables from being prosecuted in a court of law". In 1991 a doctor in Orissa was suspended for giving a false medical report during the trial in which a tribal woman living near Baripada alleged she had been raped[61].

Because of the widely reported falsifications in post-mortem reports, relatives have sometimes sought to have post-mortem examinations carried out in a hospital outside the area in which the death occurred. The father of Prakash Kamble sought by legal action to ensure that the post-mortem on his son should not be conducted at the Thane hospital because of fears that the police might manipulate its findings. It was carried out at JJ hospital in Bombay and concluded that the cause of death was shock following multiple injuries. In other cases, relatives have pressed for a second examination, and sometimes, as in the case of Sodarraj Thangraj, who died in custody in Santa Cruz, Bombay, on 1 March 1988, this has resulted in detailed evidence of multiple injuries which contradicts the official post-mortem findings.

However, it is usually extremely difficult for families to obtain access to post-mortem reports, which is often a crucial first step in seeking redress. Lawyers have also told Amnesty International that they are usually denied access to post-mortem reports unless the courts grant them specific permission. The Department of Forensic

Medicine stated in May 1988 that post-mortem reports are not public documents and relatives of the deceased have no right to them. The High Court of Delhi had previously made a similar ruling[62].

Official practice, however, does seem to vary from state to state: the Chief Secretary of the Punjab government, for example, informed Amnesty International in September 1991 that "In the event of death in Jail, ... the relatives of the deceased prisoners are entitled under the rules to get a copy of the post-mortem report". The Tamil Nadu government, on the other hand, informed the lawyer petitioning the Supreme Court about the death in custody of Sekar, a *dalit*, that "the post-mortem certificate cannot be termed as a public document and consequently nobody can claim it as a matter of right either to inspect or obtain copy of the post-mortem certificate or inquiry report". Indeed, when the relatives of Sekar tried to obtain copies of these documents they were refused access to them under paragraph 177 of the Tamil Nadu (Madras) Police Standing Orders.

4

Why the police use torture

The main reason why torture continues to be practised on such a wide scale throughout India is that the police feel themselves to be immune — they are fully aware that they will not be held accountable, even if they kill the victim and even if the truth is revealed. Institutional factors which contribute to the persistence of torture include: the negative public image and bad working conditions of the police, the inadequate training and facilities available to them, the high degree of political involvement in directing their activities and the failure of the government to accept responsibility for ensuring that the police operate within the limits of the law.

The police in India enjoy only a low level of public confidence and respect. In a comment that epitomizes public perceptions, *The Statesman* in September 1989 observed that "...irrespective of the ruling party's professed ideology, the police remains, in the words of an Allahabad High Court judge, the most organized group of criminals in India". Indeed, some police officers have expressed similar concerns themselves. A Haryana head constable complained in October 1991: "we are shunned by the public we are supposed to protect"[63].

Recommendations for police reforms, such as those proposed by the National Police Commission since 1979, have been consistently ignored by successive central and state governments. Upendra Baxi, Vice-Chancellor of Delhi University and a noted analyst of police behaviour, states that the police remain an "exploited, neglected and despised minority" who are denied the most basic minimum working conditions and who are "subservient to the rulers rather than responsive to the people". The police are poorly paid, suffer difficult working conditions, lack adequate housing and have little job security. The police have no rights of association under the Police Forces (Restriction of Rights) Act 1966.

These conditions led to a police revolt in Haryana state in mid-1991. A leader of the unofficial Haryana Police Association said "We are the lowest paid among the government employees, misused by politicians and officials alike, run around for twenty-four hours and earn finally not two square meals but a bad name from the public"[64]. After conducting a series of interviews of senior police officials in June 1988, *The Statesman* reported: "Undoubtedly many of the excesses committed by the police are due to a tremendous degree of frustration in the lower rungs of the force".

Central to the demands of the Haryana police was freedom from improper political influence and interference, which is alleged to be present in all aspects of police operations from recruitment to methods of investigation. "We are pawns in the hands of the powerful politicians and clever officers...", the leader of the Haryana police said. Earlier, a senior police officer was quoted as saying that "... out of nearly 8,000 station house officers in India, practically two-thirds are political appointees whose main job is to make money and give part of it to their political patrons to keep them happy"[65]. The NPC also confirmed this practice: "It is common knowledge now that postings of officers at this level are rarely left to the district Superintendent of Police but are regulated by instructions, mostly oral and sometimes written, from the Government"[66]. The Andhra Pradesh Police Association, in a resolution adopted at its annual meeting in October 1986, specifically attributed deaths in custody to such political interference, as did two opposition members of the Maharashtra legislative assembly during a July 1991 debate on custodial deaths.

This problem has long been recognized. The NPC concluded that such prevalent political interference often resulted in "discretionary enforcement of the law while dealing with public order situations, with emphasis on severity and ruthlessness in regard to persons opposed to the ruling party". In September 1988 a former Director of the National Police Academy in Hyderabad wrote: "It now seems to be taken for granted that...the police, would be available to the ruling party to protect its supporters, to harass its opponents, and to further its political interests.... In many places the politicians, the police and lumpen elements have developed a vested interest. For the policeman who joins this combine it is both a means of enrichment and an insurance against punishment if exposed"[67].

The National Police Commission has analyzed how, in post-independence India, political interference over the police was fostered by the long sustained rule of one political party, the Congress Party: "Prolonged one-party rule at the Centre and in the States for over 30 years coupled with the natural desire of ruling partymen to remain in positions of power resulted in the development of [a] symbiotic relationship between politicians on [the] one hand and the civil services on the other. Vested interests grew on both sides. What started as a normal interaction between the politicians and the services for the avowed objective of better administration ... soon degenerated into different forms of intercession, intervention and with malafide objectives unconnected with public interest"[68].

Police organization is still structured on the 1861 Police Act, Section 23 of which requires a police officer "promptly to obey and execute all orders and warrants lawfully issued to him by any competent authority". This allows civil and political executives authority to control the police. As Upendra Baxi concluded in a study of the India legal system: "No wonder 'third degree' methods prevail ... since the order to use them on suspects in police custody comes from such 'competent' authority (including not infrequently from the Superintendent of Police...)."[69] At its 1986 annual meeting, the Andhra Pradesh police said that most custodial deaths were due to pressure on police to detect crime from senior officers and the local ruling party.

More recently, in May 1991, the former inspector general of police in Tamil Nadu gave the following explanation: 'When the police are pressurised to deliver results when they don't have adequate time or manpower to devote to crime investigations they take short cuts to achieve their ends. In this process violations of fundamental rights do occur'."

Concern that inadequate police training contributes to custodial violence is also long-standing, but again recommended improvements have not been implemented. Officials have similarly complained that a total lack of modern investigative techniques contributes to police excesses. In 1988 S.N. Roy, then Director General of the Bihar police, said he totally disapproved of torture but pointed out that the police were not encouraged to use other methods, and that they lacked training in modern, scientific techniques of interrogation.

Article 246 of the Constitution assigns responsibility for the police to the state governments. Through their superiors — headed by the director general of police — the police report to the state home minister. At the same time, central government also has important constitutional responsibilities for the police and wide powers to influence their performance and behaviour. These include the recruitment and management of the most senior police officers belonging to the Indian Police Service (IPS), the promotion of police research and the development of professional training institutions. Police agencies such as the Central Bureau of Investigation (CBI), the Central Reserve Police Force (CRPF) and the Border Security Force (BSF) report directly to the central government Ministry of Home Affairs. Article 355 of the Constitution requires the central government to protect states against both external aggression and internal disturbance. This provision has also been used in non-emergency situations to deploy paramilitary forces, such as the BSF and the CRPF, to assist the police in areas affected by armed opposition. Most importantly, although the funding of the police is a state expenditure, the central government has powers to ensure that adequate resources are allocated to policing and to provide additional financial support.

The central government bears a large measure of responsibility for the misbehaviour of the police because of its long-standing failure to ensure that adequate resources are allocated to their training and operation. Between 1979 and 1981 the NPC made a series of well thought-out and detailed recommendations relating to the selection of police officers, their training, supervision, working conditions and pay, and proposed an effective machinery to investigate human rights violations by the police. It also recommended that a special unit should be created in the Home Ministry to examine and implement these recommendations. However, the central government has so far failed to implement the NPC's recommendations or take any other effective steps to halt torture, rape and other forms of custodial violence. Instead, it has simply denied to the international community that these violations occur, and insisted that effective remedies exist for anyone who wishes to complain about it.

5

Remedies

"One of the fundamental requisites of good government in a democracy is an institutionalised arrangement for effectively guarding against excesses or omissions by the executive in the exercise of their powers or discharge of their mandatory duties which cause injury, harm, annoyance or undue hardship to any individual citizen. This arrangement has not only to include internal checks and balances to minimise the scope for such misconduct but also to ensure an effective inquiry into any specific complaint of an alleged excess or omission and expose it promptly for corrective as well as penal action. This is specially necessary in the police who have vast scope for exercise of powers by a large number of personnel affecting the rights and liberty of individual citizens in daily life."

Thus, the National Police Commission set out the institutional framework and preconditions for an effective redress machinery against police abuses[70]. This chapter examines existing legal safeguards designed to protect detainees against police excesses and to provide redress to victims of violations. It also reviews the application of these safeguards, and examines why the existing machinery fails to provide effective redress, especially when the victims are poor and underprivileged. As the late Prime Minister, Rajiv Gandhi, acknowledged, "thousands wait while an elaborate and arcane machinery grinds ever so slowly. The poor have little hope of timely redress"[71].

The law

On paper, the laws guarding against excesses

are substantial. The Constitution protects the right to life and personal liberty (Article 21) and other fundamental rights. Although the prohibition of torture in specific terms lacks constitutional authority, Indian courts have held that Article 21 implies protection against torture and that Sections 330 and 331 of the Indian Penal Code (IPC), as well as Section 29 of the Indian Police Act, specifically forbid the practice[72]. Rape of a woman in police custody carries an enhanced punishment of 10 years' imprisonment under Section 376 of the IPC, which also extends the same punishment to public servants, such as members of the armed forces. In cases of death in custody, an inquiry by a magistrate is mandatory under Section 176 of the Code of Criminal Procedure (CCP).

The right to enforce the human rights provided in the Constitution is itself constitutionally protected. Article 226 empowers the high courts (there are 17 in India) to issue writs for the enforcement of such rights, including *habeas corpus*. Article 32 of the Constitution grants the same powers to the Supreme Court. Although a direct approach to the Supreme Court is guaranteed, the court has often in practice required victims to approach a high court first. A victim can also bring a civil suit for damages under the Civil Procedure Code, or initiate a criminal prosecution.

The practice

The laws are enforced by a judiciary with a strong tradition of independence. Although heavily overworked and dealing with a vast backlog of cases resulting in delays of many years[73], judges, especially of the higher courts, have from time to time given far reaching and innovative decisions. Two outstanding decisions enhancing the detainees' rights are described below.

In *Nandini Satpathy vs P.L. Dani*[74], the Supreme Court held that an accused has the right to consult a lawyer during interrogation and that the right not to make self-incriminatory statements should be widely interpreted to cover the pre-trial stage of police investigations. The court criticized the police for calling women to police stations for investigation saying this constituted a violation of section 160(1) of the CCP, which requires the police to interview males under 15 and women in the place where they reside.

In a 1983 case brought by journalist Sheela Barse against the state of Maharashtra[75], the Supreme Court directed the state government to produce pamphlets in local languages setting out the rights of arrested persons. These pamphlets were to be placed in each police cell and to be read out to all detainees on their arrival at a police station. The police were instructed to inform the nearest Legal Aid Committee immediately of an arrest so that the committee might provide assistance at once, at government expense. The police are also to inform relatives immediately of an arrest. Women detainees are to be kept separate from male detainees and a female officer is to be present during the interrogation of women detainees. The Supreme Court also directed city and sessions judges to make unannounced visits to police stations to check on the treatment of inmates. Finally, the court directed magistrates before whom detainees appear always to inquire whether they had complaints of police torture, and to inform all detainees that they have a right to a medical examination under Section 54 of the CCP. However, these excellent directives have not been implemented by the vast majority of officials, police and magistrates to whom they were addressed.

Equally important decisions have been given by some high courts, notably the Guwahati High Court, which has jurisdiction over all seven northeast states. It has repeatedly intervened to protect victims of torture and ill-treatment. The court has upheld numerous *habeas corpus* petitions and ordered that detainees be brought before it. Some were subsequently released on bail and, in several cases where torture was alleged, the court ordered that medical examinations be carried out.

In March 1988 the Guwahati High Court took an historic step when it itself initiated a public interest action and began legal proceedings against the Assam government on the basis of newspaper accounts of a police inquiry into a rape case in Kokrajhar district.

The victims were several teenage tribal girls who had been gang-raped in January 1988 by Assam police officers. Both the police and the Assam government denounced the allegations as "false and baseless". However, following public pressure, the Assam government ordered a high level inquiry and, after the High Court judgment, a judicial inquiry. Nine police officers, including a sub-inspector, were suspended and charged, and eight of them were arrested on 10 March. The High Court also ordered the Assam government to make an *ex-gratia* payment to the victims, pending the conclusion of these investigations.

In March 1991 the Guwahati High Court took significant steps to restrain the army from torturing women, when it ruled that women must not be taken to army camps for interrogation or any other purpose. The court also directed both the central and the Assam governments to instruct all army officers promptly that all detainees must be transferred to the nearest police station with least possible delay, and brought before a magistrate within 24 hours of arrest.

Unfortunately, court rulings which protect the detainees' rights remain the exception to the rule. Faced with the reality that the vast majority of the Indian population are unaware of their rights and lack the financial and other resources to exercise them, imaginative civil rights and judicial activists invented the concept of public interest litigation. This is a public redress system unique to India. It cuts through the usual lengthy and costly legal formalities by allowing the poorest victims of human rights abuses to approach the Supreme Court directly, or if the victim cannot do so him or herself, through a *bona fide* organization or person. The Supreme Court has even acted on a simple letter or postcard written by a prisoner. The Supreme Court's judgment in the Sheela Barse case resulted from a letter the journalist had written to the court complaining of custodial violence to which women were subjected in Bombay police stations.

However, public interest litigation is now less often used for a number of reasons. These include the inability of the Supreme Court to deal with such cases because of a lack of resources, the disinclination or inability of many judges to hear them or give such cases priority, and the small number of lawyers concerned to use the potential it provides for effective human rights protection. Perhaps the most important reason, however, is the lack of official support.

Inquiries

The first prerequisite for any meaningful redress is to establish the truth about what happened through an effective inquiry into specific complaints of custodial violence. Often, that does not happen.

Investigations can be held by the police or security forces themselves, by local magistrates or by a judicial authority. When the police conduct their own inquiries, they are not perceived as independent. Often, they absolve the police. A comprehensive survey by the NPC of some 68,275 complaints investigated by the police substantiated allegations of police misconduct in only seven per cent of the cases[76].

Although a magisterial inquiry is a legal requirement whenever a person dies in the custody of the police, the security forces or prison authorities, such inquiries are often not held. Amnesty International found that inquiries by a magistrate were held in only 42 of the 415 cases of deaths in custody it has documented since 1985[77]; another 39 inquiries were ordered to be held. West Bengal and Andhra Pradesh are states in which a relatively high number of judicial and magisterial inquiries have been conducted into allegations of torture and custodial deaths. Even so, when Chief Minister Jyoti Basu announced in April 1989 that all cases of custodial deaths in West Bengal were being investigated, he was contradicted a month later by the Calcutta Police Commissioner, who admitted that inquiries had been held in only five of the 17 deaths which had occurred in the state in the previous five years.

Amnesty International's own research confirms this pattern. Of 43 cases in West Bengal reported since 1985 inquiries by a magistrate were reported in five and judicial inquiries in one. The PUDR investigated 30 cases of custodial deaths in Delhi between 1985 and mid-1991: in only 18 cases were inquiries held by magistrates, and no more than 12 had been completed and sent to the lieutenant-governor for action. Relatives and civil liberties groups have complained that it is difficult to obtain access to reports of such magisterial inquiries.

Official statistics about deaths in prison confirm that statutory obligations to hold inquiries by magistrates are not met and that their reports are often not accessible to the public. On 24 October 1991 the Minister of State for Home Affairs, M.M. Jacob, said he was concerned about the rising number of deaths — 106 — which had occurred in New Delhi's Tihar Jail since 1988. Most causes of death cited were sickness and suicide but inquest reports had only been finalised in 48 cases — none of them reportedly with adverse reference to jail officials. In the other 58 cases, the reports were "still awaited". In a few cases, they were "untraceable".

The legally mandatory inquiry into custodial deaths can be held either by an executive magistrate (a member of the civil service appointed by the state government and under executive control) or by a judicial magistrate (a judicial official, independent of the executive). In practice, most inquiries are conducted by executive magistrates. They are often inconclusive: executive magistrates have limited powers of investigation and must rely on evidence provided by the police. They are also subject to police pressure. Their inquiries are not commonly perceived as independent and impartial. Public opinion often demands instead a judicial inquiry, widely believed to be the most authoritative, independent and impartial type of investigation. A high percentage of judicial inquiries have effectively established police culpability. However, officials tend to avoid judicial inquiries, a state minister in Karnataka dismissing them in 1988 as "time consuming and unnecessary". Instead, what usually happens, according to *The Statesman*, 4 August 1989, is:

> *"The demand for a judicial probe is easily reconciled with the one by an executive magistrate. The dependants of the victim are soon left alone to make a statement before the inquiring magistrate. The police and their henchmen remain at liberty to play tricks upon the family distraught by the loss. The political parties conveniently forget that the magistracy is another arm of the Government that is only too fond of working in tandem with the police. This phenomenon has been laid bare time and again and one never hears of the outcome of the protracted magisterial inquiries into such cases. The guilty policemen are taken as a part of the official fraternity and invariably rejoin the force after spending a few months in oblivion."*

Unfortunately, judicial inquiries into custodial deaths are rarely held: Amnesty International found they were held in only 11 and ordered in another seven of the 415 cases it has documented. The highest number was recorded in Andhra Pradesh where eight of the 31 custodial deaths documented in the state since 1985 resulted in judicial inquiries. The outcome of one case is not known to Amnesty International, but in five of the other cases the inquiries found evidence that the victims had died in police custody after torture. In a seventh case the judge found evidence of a police assault but was unable to conclude who was responsible for causing the victim's death. In the remaining case the investigating judge concluded that death was not the result of torture but noted irregularities in the conduct of the inquest, which had been held by the police instead of a magistrate, and in the post-mortem examination.

The reports of judicial inquiries in Andhra Pradesh were thorough and of high quality, no doubt because they were conducted by senior judicial officials who have stronger powers to investigate. These must include, according to an inquiry report by Justice A.D.V. Reddy. "... all the powers necessary for summoning witnesses, procuring documents, receiving evidence on affidavits, issuing Commissions for the examination of witnesses, utilising the services of certain officers and investigating agencies for conducting investigation with regard to a particular aspect or problem relevant to the inquiry"[78].

It is not surprising that, with such investigative tools at their disposal, judicial inquiries have resolved a much higher number of cases of custodial death than magisterial inquiries. The NPC drew the same conclusion regarding torture complaints in general: "Analysis of complaints of police torture dealt with in [eight states] in 1977 shows that 82 complaints were dealt with by magisterial inquiries, 17 by judicial inquiries and 430 by inquiries by other agencies like state C.I.D., Vigilance, etc. Number of instances in which police were held to blame were 37 out of 82 magisterial inquiries, 11 out of 17 judicial inquiries and 23 out of 430 inquiries by other agencies. Percentage of inquiries which disclosed actionable material is highest in the case of judicial inquiries, lower in magisterial inquiries and lowest in inquiries conducted by other agencies"[79].

The NPC's detailed study of the techniques available to investigate complaints against the police led it to recommend that judicial inquiries should be mandatory and held promptly in all cases of "alleged rape of a woman in police custody" and "death or grievous hurt caused while in police custody"[80]. Had that recommendation been implemented many would not have been raped or tortured to death by the police.

Compensation

On a July morning in 1988, a 26-year-old teacher named Kalpana Sumathi was found half naked, unconscious and bleeding near the police station in Thally, Tamil Nadu. She had been missing for 16 hours. She was taken to hospital where she was found to have 21 injuries, including several deep cuts to the head, a partially severed ear lobe, extensive cuts and abrasions on her back and serious injuries to her hands which appeared to have been slashed repeatedly.

Regaining consciousness, Kalpana Sumathi said that she had been abducted by a police employee, and then gang-raped by four police officers, and that most of her injuries were sustained when she tried to resist. She was hospitalized for three weeks. News of her rape provoked widespread public protest. An inquiry was carried out by a magistrate, who examined 17 witnesses, including doctors who had treated her. On the basis of the magistrate's report the Tamil Nadu government ordered the prosecution of the four police officers accused of the rape, and the transfer of a further seven. All four police officers were granted bail.

A Madras-based lawyer read about Kalpana Sumathi's plight in the press and on 18 September 1988 filed a public interest petition in the Supreme Court demanding compensation for Kalpana Sumathi, and for a comprehensive scheme of redress and rehabilitation for all victims of rape by members of the police and security forces. The court awarded Kalpana Sumathi Rs 20,000 (the claim was for Rs 100,000) as interim compensation, and left her to claim for further compensation once the trial of the police was over. But she could not do so: two years later charges against the police had still to be drawn up and numerous hearings had been adjourned. By then Kalpana Sumathi had spent Rs 40,000 on medical treatment alone, twice the sum the Supreme Court had awarded her. She said: "I suffer from dizziness every day.... I am suffering from 75 per cent disability in my hands.... I am not able to do any ordinary work with them and am dependant on others". She petitioned the Supreme Court again in November 1990 requesting expedition of the police officers' trial so that she could claim full compensation and at least recover the costs of medical treatment necessary to restore the use of her hands[81]. To date, however, she is still waiting for their trial to start.

Successive Indian governments have persistently resisted all attempts to establish the right to monetary compensation for wrongful actions by their agents and officers. They have argued that the state is not liable for the acts of its officers when discharging "sovereign functions". They have also failed to act on the 1956 Law Commission's recommendation that state liability should be the rule and "sovereign immunity" the exception. Moreover, the government has made an express reservation to Article 9 of the ICCPR by stating that "there is no enforceable right to compensation for persons claiming to be victims of unlawful arrest or detention against the State". As a result, Indian courts have traditionally been reluctant to award compensation to victims of human rights violations.

This position has improved in recent years. In the 1981 Bhagalpur blindings case the Supreme Court held the state liable for acts of its servants even if they acted beyond their authority. In 1983 the Supreme Court ruled that a person whose right to life and personal liberty has been violated by the state is entitled to compensation which can be awarded both in a *habeas corpus* petition and a civil suit for damages[82]. Three years later the Supreme Court awarded compensation to a member of the Jammu and Kashmir state legislative assembly who was arrested and illegally detained. In awarding Bhim Singh Rs 50,000 for the wrongful deprivation of his liberty, the court said: "If the personal liberty of a Member of the Legislative Assembly is to be played with in this fashion, one can only wonder at what may happen to lesser mortals! Police officers who are custodians of the law and order should have the greatest respect for the personal liberty of the citizen and should not flout the laws by stooping to such bizarre acts of lawlessness"[83]. In 1989 the Supreme Court awarded Rs 75,000 compensation to Mrs Kamlesh Kumari whose nine-year-old son was beaten to death by Delhi police officers[84]. This is the first known judgment in which the Supreme Court explicitly ruled that the state is liable to pay compensation to the victims of police misconduct.

Relatives of people killed in custody by the police have found it particularly hard to obtain compensation, not only because torture is hard to prove — the police usually being the only witnesses — but also because of state claims of "sovereign immunity". Usually, all the government does is to announce a small payment to the family. When Mohan Singh, who had a wife and two children, was beaten to death in a Rajasthan police station, the state did not dispute the death and announced in May 1987 it would give Rs 2,000 to the family. The matter would have rested there if a legislator had not written to the Supreme Court to say the amount was ridiculously low. The Rajasthan government claimed "sovereign immunity" from any obligation to pay the victims, but offered an *ex gratia* payment of Rs 30,000. The Supreme Court increased the amount to Rs 100,000.

In 1987 a court in Kerala ordered, perhaps for the first time, that the relatives of victims of custodial deaths should be compensated. It awarded compensation to the parents of a 26-year-old man named Bhuvanendran who had died in police custody seven years earlier. Although a sessions court in Andhra Pradesh had dismissed a civil claim for damages on grounds of "sovereign immunity", the Andhra Pradesh High Court, on appeal, held the state directly liable for deaths in police and judicial custody. In granting damages in 1989 to Ramakrishna Reddy, whose father had been killed in jail by personal rivals, the Andhra Pradesh High Court held: "Where a citizen has been deprived of his life or liberty otherwise than in accordance with the procedure established by law, it is no answer to say that the said deprivation was brought about while the officials of the State were acting in discharge of the sovereign functions of the State"[85].

Yet very few courts have granted compensation to the relatives of people tortured to death by the police. Amnesty International's survey of 415 case shows that compensation was ordered in only 12 cases, and in only six of these is payment known to have been made.

Civil suits and private criminal complaints

The government has argued that victims of police excesses have the opportunity to bring a civil suit for damages or to initiate a criminal complaint. However, civil claims involve such lengthy and costly procedures that very few use them and complaints against the police are rarely successful. In the case of Ramakrishna Reddy cited above, the Andhra Pradesh High Court dismissed civil claims as an ineffective means of redress: "A civil remedy is a case of chasing a mirage and criminal action is no solace".

Despite tremendous obstacles some victims or their relatives have pursued such action. It took 14 years of litigation in a civil suit for the parents of P. Rajan to receive Rs 372,000 compensation in 1990. The police had persistently denied Rajan's arrest but the Kerala High Court disbelieved the police, accepted evidence from witnesses to his arrest, and issued a *habeas corpus* writ after which the police, unable to produce him in court, admitted that Rajan had died in police custody under torture.

Very few civil suits against the police are successful. Wilson, a balloon seller, died in the custody of the Delhi police in 1984. A private criminal complaint was brought against the police the same year and in 1987 police officers were summoned to face trial for murder, unlawful detention and torture. Lawyers for the police have repeatedly asked for adjournments and raised legal objections against the prosecutions: eight years later the charges against the accused police officers have still not been drawn up.

Archana Guha, a torture victim, has been struggling to obtain justice and compensation since 1977, but has not yet succeeded. A headmistress of a junior high school in Calcutta, capital of West Bengal, she was arrested in July 1974, in place of her brother who was wanted by the police on suspicion of involvement with the *Naxalites*. She was hung from a pole by her hands and feet, beaten, kicked, burned with cigarettes and threatened with rape at Calcutta police headquarters. Although she was never charged or brought to trial, she remained in jail for three years. The torture she suffered caused paralysis of her legs and she left the jail in a wheelchair in May 1977. Soon after her release, Archana Guha began court proceedings to bring to justice those guilty of her torture.

Fourteen years later, they have still not been brought to justice. The officer in charge, who has since been promoted, has reportedly sought to use every legal avenue to keep the case out of court. In 1988 the Calcutta High Court quashed the case on the grounds that it had exceeded the time limit on criminal cases, even though Archana Guha had yet to give evidence in court. Her appeal against that ruling was allowed, on the grounds that those accused of torturing her had "at every stage" taken "steps which prolonged and intended to frustrate the proceedings". Since then a further array of applications for "stay orders" have impeded any progress towards bringing the police officers who tortured Archana Guha to justice.

Her case and those of the many others described in this report demonstrate the need for the Indian government to take urgent and drastic steps to halt torture and provide a speedy and effective redress mechanism for the victims of gross and persistent human rights violations in India.

6

10-point program to combat torture

Amnesty International recommends that the following steps be taken to enhance the protection of human rights in India, halt the practice of torture and create an effective institutional framework for the prevention of torture and other violations of human rights.

1. Adopt an official policy to protect human rights

The government should publicly acknowledge that torture is used as a routine method of interrogation and intimidation in police stations and other places of detention. It should make the combat of torture an issue of high priority to which the entire nation should be committed.

All political parties should adopt such a policy and implement it in the states where they are in power.

2. Investigate impartially all allegations of torture

Judicial inquiries should be made mandatory into all allegations of torture, including rape, and deaths in custody. The government should ensure that *prima facie* reports of torture, rape and deaths in custody published by the news media and by civil liberties groups are promptly and effectively investigated by an independent and impartial body.

The judges should have all necessary resources and powers to carry out their investigations effectively, including powers to compel witnesses to attend and to obtain documentary evidence.

Witnesses should be protected from intimidation and harassment and those accused of torture suspended from duty during such inquiries.

The inquiries should be conducted within a reasonable time and the results should immediately be made public. Special care should be taken to protect poor and illiterate victims who lack access to existing redress mechanisms.

The Supreme Court and the high courts should conduct their own inquiries whenever a victim alleges torture or illegal detention in a *habeas corpus* petition. In all cases where detainees are brought before the lower courts in a condition indicating they were or may have been tortured, such courts should inquire into the date of arrest, the identity of those responsible for arrest and detention, and the physical condition of the detainee. Such detainees should immediately be sent for a medical examination by an independent doctor.

All detainees should have the right to a medical examination promptly after admission to the place of custody and regularly thereafter, and to be examined by a doctor of their choice. Prompt medical examinations, by a female doctor wherever possible, are of crucial importance to women who allege they have been raped: it is virtually the only way in which rape can be authoritatively proved or disproved.

3. Bring the perpetrators to justice

The government should make a public commitment that torture or ill-treatment of detainees in custody of the police or security forces will not be tolerated and that it will ensure that such abuses will invariably lead to the perpetrators being brought to justice. It should issue directives to all concerned authorities at the central and state levels that torture is forbidden under any circumstances, as stipulated in Article 4 of the International Covenant on Civil and Political Rights.

The government should create effective systems whereby members of the police and the security forces will be held accountable for acts of torture. Legal provisions in Section 6 of the Armed Forces Special Powers Act granting the security forces immunity from prosecution, and provisions inhibiting prosecutions of police officers — such as exist under section 197 of the Code of Criminal Procedure — should be abolished.

Victims, their legal representatives and their relatives who wish to prosecute police officials for criminal offences and/or sue for compensation should have a legally protected right of access to all relevant documentary evidence including police and other official records. They should also have the right of access to post-mortem reports.

The government should consider appointing special prosecutors charged with supervising and, if necessary, initiating prosecutions of police and security forces personnel.

4. Strengthen safeguards against torture

The government should ensure that existing legal safeguards are respected in all circumstances, notably the rules that all detainees be produced before a magistrate within 24 hours of arrest and that women and children are not taken to police stations for purposes of investigation. The latter rule should be extended to include other places of interrogation such as army camps.

The police should be given strict instructions to keep up-to-date centrally maintained registers of arrests and to promptly inform relatives of an arrest and the detainee's transfer.

The legal machinery to combat torture should be strengthened. The prohibition of torture and other cruel, inhuman or degrading treatment or punishment should be incorporated in the Constitution.

Access to relatives and lawyers should be prompt. The United Nations (UN) Basic Principles on the Role of Lawyers specify that lawyers should have access to detainees within 48 hours of arrest. The duty to disobey superior orders to inflict torture — as provided in Article 5 of the UN Code of Conduct for Law Enforcement Officials — should be incorporated in relevant legal instruments, especially the Indian Police Act.

The right of detainees to have access to a medical examination, to request a judge or other independent body to order a second medical examination, and for victims of torture and their legal representatives to have access to the results of any medical examinations should be incorporated in law. Families of those who die in police custody should have the right to insist that a medical or other qualified person nominated by the family is present at the post-mortem.

The government should draw up detailed guidelines for the interrogation of suspects and publish them after consulting with lawyers, bar associations, civil liberties groups and medical professional groups. It should review these guidelines periodically in consultation with these groups to ensure that they are and remain an effective mechanism to prevent torture. Special rules should be drawn up to protect particularly vulnerable groups from custodial violence. Female detainees should be kept separate from male detainees and a female officer should always be present during their interrogation.

The government should allow independent bodies to regularly inspect all places where detainees are held. It could consider granting access to police stations by local judges to make unannounced visits or grant such access to representatives of citizen's committees. It should allow the International Committee of the Red Cross (ICRC) access to all areas where there is armed conflict between the security forces and opposition groups, notably Jammu and Kashmir, Punjab and the northeast states, where the rights of detainees are now most at risk. The ICRC should be allowed to carry out its traditional activities of visiting detainees.

5. Inform detainees of their rights

The officers in charge of police stations should be instructed that all detainees must be formally notified of their rights. A list of the rights of all detainees in the local language should be displayed in all police cells and other prominent places in police stations. The duties of the police under Section 29 of the Indian Police Act, not to perpetrate "unwarrantable personal violence" on persons in their custody and to ensure that they are safely kept, should be similarly displayed.

6. Train the police and security forces to uphold human rights, and reform the police

The government should institute an intensive program of human rights education as a standard part of the training curriculum for all police and security forces personnel involved in the arrest, detention and interrogation of suspects. It should clearly identify actual practices amounting to torture under the Indian Police Act and other legal instruments.

The government should order a review of training methods to ensure that these fully reflect international standards. It should instruct police officers and members of the security forces that international standards which India is obliged to uphold prohibit the use of torture under any circumstances, even in situations of emergency. It should instruct all law enforcement personnel that orders from a superior officers are no defence against charges of torture. It should create incentives for those who show care to protect the rights of detainees and prisoners in their custody.

The government should undertake an urgent program of police reform, so as to create a force free from political influence and patronage. It should review and improve the conditions of service of the police as well as their right to organize and express themselves, enabling them to enhance standards of professional practice and resist improper interference by political and other local forces. It should examine and implement without further delay the relevant recommendations for police reform and investigation into police misconduct made in the seven reports of the National Police Commission 1979-1981.

7. Compensate the victims
There should be a statutory right to compensation. An effective machinery for redress for victims of torture and ill-treatment, including rape, and custodial deaths should be established. Legal aid for the victims of abuses or their families should be easily available enabling them to sue for compensation. Because of the legal and practical difficulties in obtaining timely and adequate compensation, the government could establish special tribunals solely charged with the allocation of prompt and adequate compensation to all victims of human rights violations. It should be paid by the appropriate state government or, in case of the army, the central government.

8. Provide torture victims with medical treatment and rehabilitation
Appropriate facilities should be created in all Indian states for the medical treatment and rehabilitation of victims of torture and cruel, inhuman and degrading treatment.

9. Investigate the causes and patterns of torture
The government should order an authoritative investigation into the causes and the pattern of torture in India and the circumstances facilitating its widespread occurrence.

If necessary, special structures and mechanisms should be established to receive reports of torture, rape and deaths in custody. These could be independent bodies in the various states formed to monitor such complaints and supervise appropriate follow-up. At the national level, an ombudsman or multi-party legislative committee could be established with the staff and facilities to investigate patterns of torture and custodial deaths and ensure their prompt and effective investigation and follow-up. These bodies should be obliged to report periodically to the public and recommend appropriate action to be taken to eliminate and prevent custodial violence.

10. Strengthen India's international human rights commitment
The government should strengthen its international commitment to prevent torture which it affirmed when it initiated and made a Unilateral Declaration against Torture in 1979. In doing so, India declared it would comply with the UN Declaration against Torture and implement its provisions through legal and other effective measures. The government should now, like an increasing number of other countries throughout the world, become a party to the UN Convention against Torture and Other Cruel, Inhuman or Degrading Treatment or Punishment. It should ratify or accede to the (first) Optional Protocol to the ICCPR, which allows individuals to complain to the Human Rights Committee for effective remedies after they have exhausted all domestic avenues for redress. The government should remove the reservations it made when acceding to the ICCPR withholding from Indian citizens the right to compensation in case of wrongful arrest or detention.

The government should respond in substance to the queries addressed to it by the UN Special Rapporteur on torture and the UN Special Rapporteur on summary or arbitrary executions. Relevant national and international bodies should be permitted free access to investigate reported human rights violations.

End notes

1 *The Telegraph*, Calcutta, 21 July 1986

[2] *Mohan Lal Sharma vs State of Uttar Pradesh*, 11 August 1988

[3] M.N. Buch, *Indian Express*, 23 May 1988

[4] *Deccan Herald*, 26 October 1988

[5] As of November 1991 these are: Jammu and Kashmir, Punjab, Assam and Meghalaya.

Chapter 1

[6] See Chapter 5

[7] E/CN.4/1990/17, page 27, para 88

[8] E/CN.4/1990/17

[9] A *lathi* is a bamboo stick.

[10] *The Telegraph*, Calcutta, 7 September 1991

[11] Formerly known as "untouchables". Mahatma Gandhi described them as *harijans*, meaning the children of God. This term is now considered to be derogatory by members of the scheduled castes. Its use has been banned in official documents by the Madhya Pradesh and Uttar Pradesh governments and dropped by several newspapers.

[12] *Bastar, Development and Democracy* PUCL, Madhya Pradesh, July 1989

[13] *The Story of Hadmatiya Adavasi Struggles in south Rajasthan*, PUDR, May 1991

[14] See Chapter 3

[15] The Press Council was formed in 1979 to uphold press freedom and improve standards of journalism.

[16] *The Independent*, London, 17 September 1991

[17] *The North East Times*, 13 December 1990

[18] *A report from the heart of darkness*, CPDR, April 1991

[19] *Army, Assam and its people*, PUDR, May 1991

[20] See Amnesty International report *"Operation Bluebird". A case study of torture and extrajudicial executions in Manipur*, October 1990 (AI Index: ASA 20/17/90)

[21] At least 11 and possibly 15 men were illegally executed by the Assam Rifles during the operation.

[22] *Human rights violations in Punjab: use and abuse of the law*, May 1991 (AI Index: ASA 20/11/91)

[23] *Response to the Indian Government's Comments on Amnesty International's report on Punjab* (AI Index: ASA 20/25/91)

Chapter 2

[24] *State vs Ram Sagar Yadav, AIR 1985, SC 416*

INDIA

[25] NPC, Fourth Report, June 1980, at 27.26

[26] Upendra Baxi, *Indian Express*, 30 March 1990

[27] See Chapter 5

[28] See Chapter 3

[29] Before death

[30] Deb Commission of Inquiry, report published by West Bengal Government press, Alipore, 1989

[31] AIR 1988, SC 1323

[32] *SC Legal Aid Committee vs State of Bihar and Others* (1991) 3 SCC 482

[33] Shock

[34] *Mohan Lal Sharma vs State of Uttar Pradesh*

[35] See Appendix I. A small number have died in prison because of alleged medical neglect.

[36] *The Telegraph*, Calcutta, 20 July 1986

Chapter 3

[37] *Hindustan Times*, 30 November 1986

[38] *Deccan Herald*, 26 October 1988

[39] See Articles 9 and 10 of the 1975 UN Declaration on the Protection of All Persons from Being Subjected to Torture and other Cruel, Inhuman or Degrading Treatment or Punishment, Principles 9 and 18 of the 1989 UN Principles on the Effective Prevention and Investigation of Extra-Legal, Arbitrary and Summary Executions and Principle 34 of the UN Body of Principles for the Protection of All Persons under Any Form of Detention or Imprisonment.

[40] Amnesty International received information that a police sub-inspector had been sentenced to life imprisonment in connection with a 1985 case of death in custody in Andhra Pradesh as this report went to press, too late to include details.

[41] See Chapter 5

[42] See *Allegations of extrajudicial killings by the Provincial Armed Constabulary in and around Meerut, 22-23 May 1987* (AI Index: ASA 20/06/87)

[43] *Indian Express*, 15 July 1991

[44] *Economic and Political Weekly*, 28 September 1991

[45] Human Rights Committee, 1040th meeting, 26 March 1991, statement summarized in CCPR/C/SR.1040 at 60 and 61

[46] CCP, Section 50

[47] CCP, Section 57

[48] CCP, Section 58

[49] IPC, Section 220

[50] CCP, Sections 154-155

END NOTES

[51] NPC, First Report at 10.1, 10.11 and Seventh Report at 50.4.

[52] See below, Medical aspects of official cover-up.

[53] NPC, Fourth report at 27.4

[54] That of T. Muralidharan in 1986, see below

[55] See *Human rights violations in Punjab: Use and abuse of the law* (AI Index: ASA 20/11/91)

[56] *The Hindu*, 9 October 1988

[57] *The Telegraph*, 20 June 1986

[58] CCP, Sections 174 and 176

[59] Section 54, CCP

[60] *The Telegraph*, 3 October 1991

[61] *The Telegraph*, 21 August 1991

[62] *State vs Gian Singh (1981) Cr.C.J. 538*

Chapter 4

[63] *Hindustan Times*, 3 October 1991

[64] *Hindustan Times*, 27 September 1991

[65] *Hindustan Times*, 26 October 1986

[66] NPC, Third Report at 22.9 and Second Report at 15.2

[67] *Indian Express*, 17 September 1988

[68] NPC, Second Report at 15.4

[69] Upendra Baxi, *The crisis of the Indian legal system*, page 104

Chapter 5

[70] NPC, First Report at 10.1

[71] *Times*, London, 30 December 1985

[72] Sections 330 and 331 IPC make "voluntarily causing hurt to extort confession" punishable by 10 years imprisonment.

[73] The *Hindustan Times* reported on 6 September 1991 that over 200,000 cases were pending in the Supreme Court, nearly 2 million in the high courts and over 20 million in the lower courts.

[74] AIR (1978) SC 1025

[75] *Sheela Barse vs State of Maharashtra* 1983 2 SCC 96

[76] NPC, First Report, 1979 at 10.2

[77] See Appendix I

[78] Report of Justice A.D.V. Reddy, 10 December 1986

[79] NPC, First Report at 10.4

[80] NPC, First Report at 10.18 and 10.19

99

INDIA

[81] *Rathinam vs Union of India and others*, 1989 Supp (2) SCC 716
[82] *Rudal Shah vs Bihar*, AIR 1984 SC (1068)
[83] *Bhim Singh vs Jammu and Kashmir*, AIR 1986 SC 494
[84] (1990) 1 SCC 422
[85] *Ramakrishna Reddy vs Andhra Pradesh*, 1989(2) Andhra Law Times, 1 (D.B.)

Appendix I

A list of 415 deaths in custody in India

(This list summarizes data about 415 people reported to have died in the custody of the police and security forces in India between 1 January 1985 and 1 November 1991. Full details on all cases are available from Amnesty International in "India: details of deaths in custody reported since 1985", AI Index: ASA 20/14/92.)

Deaths in custody in Andhra Pradesh, 1985 - 1991

Name, age, occupation	Date of death	Circumstances of arrest	Circumstances of death	Official action known
Chenappa, *dalit*	25/07/89	Arrested on charge of theft.	Died at Aluru, Kurnool district, allegedly tortured to death by police. Police claimed suicide.	
Vadde Srinivasulu	18/06/89	Villagers alleged torture.	Died in police custody at Kalyandurg.	
Pinganemi (or Penuganti) Sadhu (22)	06/10/88	Arrested 5 October. Allegedly beaten by bystanders and later by police.	Died in Srigavarapukota police station, Vizianagaram district. Police claimed suicide, others police killing.	Judicial inquiry ordered.
T. Mehabub Pasha (35)	04/10/88	Arrested 4 October. Taken to Vinukonda sub-jail.	Died in cell at Vinukonda sub-jail, Guntur district.	
Pitala Narasimha Rao, rickshaw-puller	02/10/88	Arrested 3 September with two others. Held in Vijayawada III police station.	Died in hospital, where he was taken by a relative allowed to move him from jail. Relatives alleged torture.	Inquest listed 10 to 14 body wounds. Magisterial and judicial inquiries. One policeman suspended. Police attempted to bribe relatives.
Vemula Venkatesh (25), factory worker	01/10/88	Surrendered to Osmania University police on 17 September. Police alleged detained on 30 September.	Died in hospital. Police say of tuberculosis. Press reported multiple injuries and burns.	Judicial inquiry ordered to report by 4 July 1989.

Appendix I

Name, age, occupation	Date of death	Circumstances of arrest	Circumstances of death	Official action known
Madiga Yesepu (28)	25/09/88 (approx.)		Died in Jupadu Bangla police station. Villagers alleged torture led to his suicide.	
Chatragadda Sambaiah	28/08/88	Arrested 23 August for possessing stolen property.	Died Eluru police station, West Godavari district. Police claimed suicide. Relatives threatened by police.	Judicial inquiry ordered.
Enibeera (or Enichera) Peda Venkataiah	05/04/88 or 07/04/88	Arrested between Ummadivaram and Pullalacheruvu during first week of April by police from the latter village on suspicion of child abduction.	Died on way to hospital. Police reportedly refused to register case of his death.	Superintendent of Police reportedly found prima facie evidence of torture by three policemen. Magisterial inquiry ordered.
Nimmali (or Nimmallaiah), (55), *dalit*	13/02/88	Taken to police station 11 February on charge of arson.	Died in Narsima Rayanipeta police station, Chittor district. Police say he ate a "poisonous leaf". Relatives claim was tortured to death.	Three policemen suspended.
Meghya	23/01/88	Arrested by Madikonda police. Hanamkonda police allegedly responsible for his death as a result of torture.	Died in Madikonda police station. Body, with multiple wounds, found hanging from electric transformer.	

India

Name, age, occupation	Date of death	Circumstances of arrest	Circumstances of death	Official action known
Bala Veera Reddy	23/11/87		Died at Vallur police station, Cuddapah district.	Judicial inquiry appointed on 31 December 1987.
Bikshapati (25)	30/07/87 (approx.)	Arrested 25 July by Hanamkonda police; later interrogated by Warangal police.	Found hanging from tree with multiple wounds. Relatives and local investigative team allege he was tortured.	Body cremated by police.
Krishna (22)	27/07/87 (approx.)	Arrested 27 July by police from Veerasaram on charge of burglary.	Found badly injured near Veerasaram police station; died soon afterwards.	A Sub-Inspector of Police and two constables suspended by Superintendent of Police, West Godavari.
Mohammed Saleem (20), fruit-seller	07/10/86	Arrested by Sanathnagar police on suspicion of theft. Police said he was arrested on 1 October, but relatives say he was detained earlier.	Died in Osmania General Hospital where he was taken on 3 October. Relatives say he was hit on head while trying to escape, and that wounds were not treated.	Post-mortem found "the right eye was completely swollen ...and there was haemorrhage due to injury".
C. David Raju (23)	23/09/86	Rearrested 23 September having escaped from Khammam sub-jail on 10 August.	Died in Khammam I town police station. Police claim suicide.	Post-mortem listed *ante mortem* injuries. Judicial inquiry found death due to police beating.

Appendix I

Name, age, occupation	Date of death	Circumstances of arrest	Circumstances of death	Official action known
T. Muralidharan, navy seaman	17/09/86	Taken to Vijayawada police station on 17 September.	Found hanging in Vijayawada police station with injuries. Police claimed he had committed suicide.	Judicial inquiry found interference with police records and indicted four policemen, recommending prosecution for murder.
Dasari Venkateswarlu	15/09/86	Arrested in first week of August and taken to Macherla police station.	Died in Macherla Hospital, Guntur district. Police deny arrest and detention. Fellow detainees say he was tortured.	Judicial inquiry found he had been illegally detained and was assaulted by four policemen in custody. Inquiry did not determine cause of death.
G. Yerra Sai	09/09/86 or 10/09/86		Died in Bellampa police station, Nazimabad district.	A panel was reportedly set up to investigate the death.
M. Sreenivasa	23/08/86		Died in Bellampa police station.	A panel was reportedly set up to investigate the death.
Nallabattula Parisudha Rao	21/07/86	Arrested on 21 July on suspicion of robbery.	Died at Thada police station. Police claim he died due to "chronic stomach ache".	Two policemen were suspended.

India

Name, age, occupation	Date of death	Circumstances of arrest	Circumstances of death	Official action known
U. Narasimha	10/07/86	Arrested on 1 July and kept in unacknowledged detention; police claim arrest date was 10 July.	Died in Sanjeeva Reddy Nagar police station with injuries on body which police claim were inflicted before arrest.	Judicial inquiry found evidence against five policemen. One transferred and one suspended.
Goddala Rama Rao (23), lorry cleaner	06/02/86	Arrested 5 February on suspicion of theft and child molestation. Taken to Vijayawada police station.	Died in Vijayawada II town police station. Police claimed he committed suicide by eating poisoned food given to him by "outsiders".	Judicial inquiry found death due to blows to stomach and ribs, and named five policemen as responsible.
M. Shekhar Reddy	10/12/85	Arrested 10 December. Taken to Nagarkurnool police station.	Died in hospital. Relatives claimed the body showed injuries.	Inquest held by policeman who arrested the victim. A judicial inquiry was held which exonerated the police.
Angadi Prabhakara Rao	27/04/85	Arrested on 27 April on suspicion of being in possession of stolen property.	Died in Chirala town police station. Medical report found 12 injuries on body. Police claim he committed suicide.	Judicial inquiry found killed in police custody, ordered suspension and prosecution of two police officials and a former magistrate.

Appendix I

Name, age, occupation	Date of death	Circumstances of arrest	Circumstances of death	Official action known
Bashir Ahmad (20)	24/08/91	Reportedly arrested on 23 August by Madanapalle police, and allegedly tortured in the police station.	Died either in Madanapalle police station or in hospital, allegedly due to beatings by police. The police claim he had epileptic fit.	The body allegedly showed several injuries. CB-CID and magisterial inquiries were ordered. Three police officers were suspended.
Ramesh	early September 1989	Arrested in Maharashtra on suspicion of being a Naxalite; kept in Godvarikhani police station, Karimnagar district.	Died in the police station, allegedly having committed suicide.	The Chief Minister ordered a judicial commission to investigate the alleged suicide.
Govindu (27)	19/03/89	Reportedly taken to One Town police station, Nellore. Allegedly beaten by Crime Sub-Inspector and three other Constables.	Died either in One Town police station or (as police claim) in hospital. Allegedly died due to beatings by police.	Police held an inquest. Body reportedly had injuries on hand, palm and feet. Crime Sub-Inspector suspended.
Devara Nageswara Rao (also known as Nagulu), *adivasi*	15/09/86	Arrested with two others in connection with a burglary by Macherla police in July. All three allegedly tortured by police, and he was allegedly starved.	Died in Macherla police station, after being poisoned by the police, according to those arrested with him.	Orders issued for his body to be exhumed on 24 September. The body was not found. A magisterial inquiry held. Home Minister stated that a case of murder would be filed against the police and the Chief Minister ordered a judicial inquiry.

India

Name, age, occupation	Date of death	Circumstances of arrest	Circumstances of death	Official action known
Rajaboyina Kasulu (24)	05/09/91	Arrested on 4 September in connection with an assault.	Found dead in a police cell at Gudivada. Police say he hanged himself. Locals blamed police for the death.	
Uppuleti Chandraiah	09/03/91	Arrested 5 March on suspicion of robbery. Allegedly tortured while interrogated in Husnabad police station.	Died in police station, allegedly as a result of torture. Police claim he committed suicide by hanging.	Official inquiry found evidence of death due to beating. Circle inspector suspended; civil surgeon suspended for issuing false post-mortem report. Five other police personnel reportedly facing departmental action.

Appendix I

Deaths in custody in Assam, 1985 - 1991

Name, age, occupation	Date of death	Circumstances of arrest	Circumstances of death	Official action known
Basiruddin (40)	26/06/91		Hanged in Batadrava police station. Police alleged he was beaten by locals.	
Shamburam Saikia (30), farmer	28/03/91	Arrested December 1990 by soldiers from Moukkuli. After six days handed over to police. Remanded in custody under TADA.	Reportedly tortured by army and sent to hospital by prison authorities. Shot in hospital by CRPF during disturbances. Died Guwahati Medical College Hospital.	
Chandrika Hazarika	23/03/91		Reportedly died in army custody near Dibrugarh.	
Pradeep Nath (28)	18/03/91	Arrested in Bihaguri on 31 January.	Reportedly tortured and admitted to hospital with injuries, where he died.	
Dhruvajyoti Gogoi, ULFA member	19/03/91	Arrested by army 17 March in Doomdooma, Tinsukia. *Habeas corpus* filed at Guwahati High Court.	On 19 March army handed body to police, claiming death was due to epilepsy. Photograph showed several injuries.	Post-mortem at Assam Medical College Hospital listed 28 injuries.

India

Name, age, occupation	Date of death	Circumstances of arrest	Circumstances of death	Official action known
Robin Bora (also known as Dhiren Bora), (23)	14/03/91	Arrested in Meleng Sumada, Jorhat.	Army claimed he jumped from jeep, but detainee said he was tortured to death.	
Suresh Phukan, teacher and Vice-President of Jatiya Unnayan Parishad (JUP)	13/03/91	Arrested 7 December 1990, detained under TADA in Dibrugarh.	Admitted to hospital after army torture, where he was found hanging in bathroom. Officials claim suicide.	Judicial inquiry demanded. Magisterial inquiry ordered.
Puran Rabha (50)	19/01/91		Died in army custody. Army claim suicide.	Magisterial inquiry ordered.
Dhiraj Chowdhury	01/01/91	Arrested in Bambundi, Kamrup.	Body found in well. Army claimed suicide, others said he was tortured to death.	
Jatin Gohain, businessman	30/12/90	Arrested near Arunachal Pradesh border. Taken to Demow military camp.	Reportedly tortured and taken to hospital.	
Sarat Sonowal (30) secondary school teacher	09/12/90	Arrested 30 November in Bhador Pachali. Village boy saw arrest by army. Family inquiries unanswered.	Reportedly tortured and admitted to hospital, where died. Body showed injuries.	

Appendix 1

Name, age, occupation	Date of death	Circumstances of arrest	Circumstances of death	Official action known
Bipin Gogoi, employee of Oil India Limited	between 04/12/90 and 06/12/90	Arrested by army 4 December.	Reportedly tortured and shot dead. Body handed on 6 December to police who noted injuries.	Post-mortem report recorded death due to bullet injury. Government claimed killed in encounter.
Gambhir Gogoi, tea estate employee and Secretary of Assam Jatiyabadi Yuva Chhatra Parishad (AJYCP)	between 30/11/90 and 06/12/90	Arrested by army 30 November or 1 December from home. Reportedly taken to Borjan army camp.	Body handed to police on 5 or 6 December. Army claimed died in firing, later in mine explosion. Relatives and police noted injuries.	AJYCP registered murder case.
Ravi Bhattacharya (20)	15/11/89 or 16/11/89	Arrested 13 November.	Found hanging in police station. Allegedly beaten to death.	Press report noted this was third suicide case in Paan Bazar police station.
Ratneswar Boro	20/05/89	Arrested 18 May with four others.	Died after two days of alleged torture in Tamulpur police station.	
Unnamed, village headman of Likabali	27/03/89	Arrested from farmhouse by Silapathar police.	Found dead next day by family in Assam police custody.	Arunachal Pradesh government asked for CBI inquiry.
Narendra Narzari (18)	30/12/88	Arrested in Simlaguri village when visiting relatives.	Reportedly shot dead when ordered to enter police van.	

India

Name, age, occupation	Date of death	Circumstances of arrest	Circumstances of death	Official action known
Jona Basumatary (30)	14/09/88	Arrested while collecting medicine in No. 2 Salbari village.	Reportedly killed inside a police van.	
Phanen Sumpramary (22)	21/11/87	Arrested in Ranisundri during raid by Bengtol police.	Reportedly died in Sidli police station after torture.	
Sarthelekthe, member of the People's Defence Forum	Feb. 1987	arrested by Uttarboli police who allegedly put nails in his toes at Diphy police station.	Died in Uttarborbill police station, Tarayasa Rongpi.	
Hareshwar Deka, student (22)	15/06/85	Arrested 13 June with eight others by Ambari Fatasil police.	Died next day after release. Friends claim because of torture. Police claim he committed suicide.	Post-mortem carried out, stating cause of death as asphyxiation.
Raju Baruah (20), female	06/10/91	Allegedly raped by four soldiers on 6 October.	Thrown into a pond, allegedly by soldiers; died in hospital.	One soldier identified by Raju's sisters arrested. Post-mortem indicated signs of rape. The Chief Minister granted *ex-gratia* payment to family.

112

Appendix I

Deaths in custody in Bihar, 1985 - 1991

Name, age, occupation	Date of death	Circumstances of arrest	Circumstances of death	Official action known
Gura Kumhar (35), *adivasi*	15/09/91	Arrested 15 September near Chandil by the Railway Police Force (RPF) for allegedly stealing coal. Residents alleged that he was attacked by the RPF after the RPF men had attempted to molest his wife.	He allegedly died in Bhumigpara from being beaten by the RPF.	The body was sent for post-mortem. RPF policemen allegedly threatened villagers not to inform the police about the incident.
Dwarika Thakur	04/09/91	Arrested with seven others on 4 September by police from Makhdumpur police station, Jehanabad district.	Other detainees claim that he was beaten to death by police. His body was not found.	Police inquiry conducted. The Station House officer and one inspector were suspended.
Pappu Ram *dalit*	June 1991	Arrested by members of Chutia police, Ranchi district.	Allegedly beaten to death and cremated by police in Chutia police station.	
Kameshwar Ravi	May 1991		Died in Chutia police station, allegedly killed by police officers.	

India

Name, age, occupation	Date of death	Circumstances of arrest	Circumstances of death	Official action known
Anil Lakara	20/04/91	Reportedly arrested by Lalpur police on 19 April.	Police claim he was killed in an encounter in Morabadi Grounds on the night of 20 April.	Before his death, Anil's father had filed a petition stating that his son had been arrested on 19 April. The court ordered Lalpur police to present a report by 23 April.
Sanatan Shabar, *adivasi*	21/03/91	Prisoner in Jamshedpur jail from 6 August 1990.	Died in hospital.	Cause of death: TB. According to the post-mortem, his illness was improperly treated and should not have been fatal.
Tarani Shabar (at least 70), *adivasi*	15/09/90	Arrested by Musabani police on murder charge, but his name was not on the charge sheet. He could not afford bail and remained in Jamshedpur jail.	Died in hospital.	According to the post-mortem report, he died of chronic illness and lack of food. Press reports allege he died of medical neglect.
Wilson Roy (also known as Pappu)	27/07/90	Arrested by Jagannath police on charges of robbery with two others. Allegedly beaten during arrest.	Died in Jagannath police station, allegedly beaten to death.	A magisterial inquiry found police responsible for the deaths and issued arrest warrants for murder against three police officials.
Uday Sharma	27/07/90	Arrested with Wilson Roy (See above).	See above.	See above.

Appendix I

Name, age, occupation	Date of death	Circumstances of arrest	Circumstances of death	Official action known
Johnson Kindo	28/07/90	Arrested with Wilson Roy (See above).	See above.	See above.
Nayeem	25/10/89	Picked up by police after an explosion during riots in Bhagalpur.	Allegedly shot by police.	As of April 1990 the body had not been returned to the family.
Lalji Beldar (25)	23/09/89	Arrested on 22 September by police from Phulwari Shari police station, Patna.	Allegedly beaten to death in custody. Police claim he escaped, but body never found.	An official inquiry was ordered. Police did not raise alarm about the escape, or attempt to chase him.
Basudev Ravani (55), coal miner	15/07/89	Arrested by Loyabad police. Police claim he assaulted a man while drunk.	Died in Loyabad police station, Dhanbad, allegedly as a result of torture. Police buried him without informing family.	According to police, post-mortem did not determine cause of death. A magisterial inquiry implicated the police. The Officer-in-Charge suspended.
Mahesh Mahto	11/06/89	Caught trying to rob a train and reportedly beaten by passengers and shot by a security guard. Railway police guard took him to hospital tied to the footboard of a rickshaw.	Died in hospital.	Chief Minister asked the DIG to investigate. The Supreme Court found he died of lack of prompt treatment and ordered compensation to family.

115

India

Name, age, occupation	Date of death	Circumstances of arrest	Circumstances of death	Official action known
Surendra Poddar	10/06/89	Arrested by Khajekalan police on 10 June in connection with a rape.	Died in police station, allegedly beaten to death. Police claim he hanged himself.	
Mohammad Mumtaz	08/05/89	Arrested by Barhi police in connection with communal riots in Hazaribagh in April.	Died in Barhi hospital. Police claim that he jumped from a jeep. Family claim he was killed in police custody.	A magisterial inquiry was ordered. Patna High Court ordered body to be shown to relatives. Officials said action would be taken against policemen responsible.
Ralgrihi Ram *dalit*	12/04/89	Reportedly arrested on 11 April with eight others in possession of firearms by the Buxar police and taken to either the Buxar or Dhanasoi police station. Villagers claim to have witnessed torture of three prisoners at Dhanaria police station.	Police claim he and two others were killed in an encounter near Sitchi on 12 April where their bodies were found. Villagers claim that bodies were taken to Sitchi and shot at to make it appear they were killed in an encounter.	
Bhola Ram *dalit*	12/04/89	See above.	See above.	See above.
Amar Ram *dalit*	12/04/89	See above.	See above.	See above.

Appendix I

Name, age, occupation	Date of death	Circumstances of arrest	Circumstances of death	Official action known
Ram Naresh Singh, farmer	03/04/89	Arrested on 3 April in connection with a land dispute by police from Khudabandpur and Cheria-Bariarpur police station; taken to Khudabandpur police station.	Died in hospital, allegedly as a result of torture. Body was taken to Simariaghat under police escort and cremated.	The District Magistrate ordered the arrest of five officers from the two police stations. Compensation was also promised.
Surajdeo Chamar (35), *dalit*	13/03/89	He allegedly went to investigate a brawl among members of the Bihar Military police (BMP), and was taken away by the BMP.	Villagers claim he was beaten by BMP, released, and then shot in the back. Police deny he was taken into custody, maintaining he was killed in an "encounter".	Officials reportedly presented a blanket, wheat and Rs500 to his widow as compensation.
Abdul Sattar (32)	29/01/89	Arrested on 29 January on robbery charge by Kanke police and taken to Doranda police station.	Died in hospital, allegedly due to police beatings. Police claim he was taken there after complaining of chest pains.	Police claim doctors confirmed heart failure as cause of death. Police allegedly offered a job to a member of deceased's family.
Madik Mian	01/01/89	Arrested on 30 December in connection with a brawl; taken to Simaria police station, Hazaribagh district. Transferred to Chatra jail, allegedly after being beaten by the Officer-in-Charge.	Died in hospital the next day, allegedly as a result of torture.	A five-member parliamentary inquiry committee concluded that his death was the result of beating by the Officer-in-Charge of Simaria police station, who was suspended.

India

Name, age, occupation	Date of death	Circumstances of arrest	Circumstances of death	Official action known
Shamsuddin Mian	25/12/88	Transferred from Koderm jail to hospital in Hazaribagh on 25 December, having been set fire to by three warders.	Died in hospital.	The three jail warders were reportedly suspended.
Moti Birua (25), *adivasi*	13/12/88 approx.	Arrested in connection with a murder; held in Manjhari police station, Singhboom district, and allegedly gang raped.	Police claim that she was found hanging from a tree. Others allege she was killed by police.	Post-mortem said death not consistent with hanging. A magisterial inquiry was ordered. Two police officers were suspended and a case of murder instituted.
Meghnath Kasera	19/11/88	Arrested by Ichak police on 19 November.	Died in police station, allegedly after being beaten and shot by police.	One policeman was suspended. Brother has filed a case against the police.
Nasir Hussain	02/11/88	Arrested by Jamshedpur police on 16 November in connection with a car theft. Taken to Jamshedpur; appeared in court; remanded in custody at Sakchi police station.	Died either in Bhagalpur or Hazaribagh jail; found hanging in his cell. There are allegations that he was killed by police to silence him.	An official investigation is reported to have found that he committed suicide. Two warders were suspended.
Ram Lal Tamariah (25)	31/08/88	Arrested in connection with a burglary. Taken to Telco police station.	Died in police station or (as claimed by police) in hospital. Allegedly beaten to death.	The Officer-in-Charge of Telco police station was reportedly transferred.

Appendix I

Name, age, occupation	Date of death	Circumstances of arrest	Circumstances of death	Official action known
Kokarsake Satyendra Dubey	06/07/88	Arrested by Dalloganj police on 6 July. Police claim he was drunk.	Died in hospital, allegedly due to police torture. Death certificate mentions alcohol poisoning.	Post-mortem unable to determine the cause of death, but found no wound marks on the body.
Awadhesh Kumar Yadav (16)	26/12/87	Said to have been sexually assaulted and killed by police officer after visiting his father and uncle in Buxar Central jail on 15 December.	Died in or near Buxar Central jail. Body found in a field.	
Ajoy Kumar (16)	13/08/87	Arrested by Danapur police in connection with a theft.	Died allegedly after being kicked and beaten by police.	Two policemen reportedly charged with murder.
Kanhaiya Yadav (14)	August 1987	Visited his brother in Buxar Central jail but never returned home.	Alleged to have been sexually assaulted by police and his body dumped in the river.	
Sanichar Mushahar *dalit*	21/06/87	Brought to Sasaram jail on 3 March. Admitted to hospital on 21 June. Torture alleged.	Died in hospital. Declared a victim of "flu".	A member of the jail staff reportedly said he was taken to the hospital dead.
Kishan Ram	05/06/87	A prisoner in Sasaram jail since 15 August 1985. Torture alleged.	Taken to hospital on 5 June, where he died.	

India

Name, age, occupation	Date of death	Circumstances of arrest	Circumstances of death	Official action known
Suresh Kharwar *dalit*	05/06/87	Arrested on 21 May; admitted to hospital on 5 June. Torture alleged.	Died either in Sasaram jail or in Sasaram hospital. Cause of death recorded as "flu".	
Lalmudi Chamar *dalit*	04/06/87	Brought 31 March to Sasaram jail. Sent to hospital 4 June. Torture alleged.	Died in jail hospital.	
Arvind Kumar Singh (20)	01/04/87 or 02/04/87	Arrested on 22 March for travelling on a train without a ticket; taken to Patna sub-jail.	Died in Patna sub-jail. Relatives claim his body had been disfigured.	
Yogendra Chaudhary	23/03/87	Arrested by Kadamkuan police, Patna, on 23 March. Apparently not charged.	Found dead on 27 March in a river, 25 km from Patna. Allegedly killed by police in the police station.	Inquiry by an Additional District Magistrate was ordered. The Chief Minister sent Rs20,000 to his widow.
Ishak (20)	1987	Held by Hansia police.	Died after allegedly being beaten by police. Police reportedly cut his throat to make it look like suicide.	Three policemen arrested on 30 September and their bail application was rejected. They have been charged with murder.
Mohammed Hussain	03/08/86	Arrested by Ranchi police on 2 August with two others for questioning.	Died in Hindpirhi police station, allegedly due to police torture. Received no medical attention.	The Officer-in-Charge was suspended and criminal charges were filed against the policemen involved. A grant of Rs3,000 paid to his family.

Appendix I

Name, age, occupation	Date of death	Circumstances of arrest	Circumstances of death	Official action known
Raju Rajak (also known as Machalia)	22/06/86	Arrested on 22 June with Ashok Ram, taken to Kotwali police station. Allegedly beaten, then taken to Morabadi Grounds and shot.	Police claim he was killed, along with Ashok Ram, in an "encounter" at the Morabadi Grounds.	
Ashok Ram	22/06/86	See above.	See above.	See above.
Mahendra Bin, dalit	20/06/86	Held in Patna Central Jail.	Taken to hospital on 5 June, where he died, allegedly due to police torture.	Post-mortem reportedly did not support police claim that he died of a long illness.
Nakul Bagdi (16), adivasi	23/12/85	Arrested 19 December by Sonari police; taken to hospital by police on 23 December.	Died in hospital, allegedly due to police torture. Police gave cause of death as pneumonia.	Two policemen were suspended, but later reinstated. Post-mortem said there was evidence of assault. A judicial magisterial inquiry was ordered which found in favour of the police version. Police reportedly intimidated witnesses. Case taken to Supreme Court.
Rajendra Musahar, dalit	03/07/85	Arrested with brother by Rajpur police, Bhojpur district, on 2 July, on suspicion of being Naxalites.	Died in Rajpur police station; officially an "accidental death". Villagers claim he was publicly beaten to death by police.	Police allegedly told the doctors performing the post-mortem to confirm the police version, but one of the doctors refused.

India

Name, age, occupation	Date of death	Circumstances of arrest	Circumstances of death	Official action known
Anthony Murmu (Santal Tribe)	between 19/04/85 and 22/04/85	Arrested by Sahebganj police. 15 Santals were shot by police as he was being arrested.	Body found on 22 April, allegedly with bullet injuries and signs of beating.	Petition taken to Supreme Court in 1985 asking for an inquiry and for compensation.
Pradeep Singh	30/03/85	Arrested 4 March after a road hold-up. Admitted to hospital with injuries on 29 March.	Died in police custody at Jamui, Munger district.	A magistrate's inquest found death due to multiple injuries. This was corroborated by post-mortem.
Balakhandi Yadav	January 1989	Reportedly a well-known dacoit, he was allegedly picked up in Jamuniya village in Nawal-Parasi disctrict, Nepal, by armed plainclothes Indian policemen and taken to Bihar.	Allegedly killed by Bihar police and body thrown in Balmikinagar forests.	
Hare Ram Yadav	29/09/88	Allegedly killed in jail to prevent him giving names of politicians using his services.	Died either in Bhagalpur or Hazaribagh jail; found hanging in his cell. Police claimed he committed suicide.	Post-mortem carried out. An official investigation is reported to have found that he committed suicide, but according to press reports it was inconceivable.

Appendix I

Deaths in custody in Haryana, 1985 - 1991

Name, age, occupation	Date of death	Circumstances of arrest	Circumstances of death	Official action known
Ramesh, *dalit*	August 1991, approx.	Arrested by three policemen from Ateli police post on suspicion of theft.	Body found several days later in a well. Villagers claim he was killed by police.	Ateli police reportedly refused at first to register a case when told he had not returned home. His family reportedly rejected compensation from the government.
Khurshid Ahmed (20, *adivasi*	24/08/91	Detained 19 August and held illegally at Punhana police station. Released 23 August on the orders of the Senior Superintendent of Police.	On his return home he claimed to have been tortured by police. Died later in the Civil Hospital, Gurgaon "due to [a] brain haemorrhage".	Post-mortem confirmed torture. The Head Constable was suspended and arrested for culpable homicide not amounting to murder. He was reported to be in custody.
Manpal Singh (25), *adivasi*	August 1990	Illegally detained in the investigation of a theft.	Died as a result of torture in Bhattu Kalan police station.	Station House Officer reportedly arrested.
Krishan Kumar (22)	December 1989	Arrested by Pataudi police after a complaint of theft.	Body found hanging by a rope from a ventilator.	The Superintendent of Police ordered an inquiry and suspended the sentry on watch in the police station.

123

Deaths in custody in Jammu and Kashmir, 1985 - 1991

Name, age, occupation	Date of death	Circumstances of arrest	Circumstances of death	Official action known
Mumtaz	13/09/91	Between 12 and 19 Sept. the army conducted cordon and search operations, during which Mumtaz' brother was shot dead.	Beaten to death by the army while performing the last rites for his brother.	
Khazir Mohammad Abdul Aziz	24/08/91 or 25/08/91	The two men were arrested by the security forces during a crackdown on their village on 24 August.	They died in an interrogation centre, according to official sources.	
Mohammad Ashraf	July 1991	Arrested by security forces during counter insurgency operations and taken to an interrogation centre.	On 18 July his body was taken home, reportedly showing signs of torture.	
Ghulam Mohammad	July 1991	Detained by the security forces and taken to an interrogation centre.	Body was handed over to relatives on 18 July.	
Abdul Gani Khan	03/12/90	Detained on 3 December by the security forces.	Body was found in Habak village. Locals said he had died in custody.	Official announced an investigation.

Appendix I

Name, age, occupation	Date of death	Circumstances of arrest	Circumstances of death	Official action known
Imtiaz Ahmed Mir (30)	October 1990	Arrested in October in Anantnag by the Central Reserve Police Force (CPRF), 53rd battalion.	The next day his body was found by a roadside, marked by torture and a bullet wound.	Relatives filed a complaint with the police. The CRPF denied his arrest.
Bashir Ahmad	11/07/90	Arrested with two others on 10 July by the security forces.	Died in custody reportedly of torture. Police refused to take his body, which was thrown into a river by security forces.	
Ghulam Hassan Sheikh	11/07/90	Arrested by the security forces on 10 July.	Died the following day reportedly of torture during interrogation.	
Fayaz Ahmad Mattoo (19)	21/06/90	Shot while bathing in a pond, then detained by CRPF; taken to an interrogation centre.	Two days later his body was returned to relatives without explanation.	
Mangta Khan	03/06/90 or 04/06/90	Arrested by the army with other villagers on 3 June and taken to an army camp.	The following day his dead body was taken to hospital, reportedly with a fractured skull.	
Ghulam Qadir War (65)	June 1990	Arrested by the security forces and taken to Akhnoor interrogation centre, Jammu.	Died in custody and despite a court order his body was not returned to his home for burial.	

India

Name, age, occupation	Date of death	Circumstances of arrest	Circumstances of death	Official action known
Mohammad Sultan Malik	June 1990	Arrested by the security forces and taken to an interrogation centre.	Died reportedly of torture.	
1. Ashiq Hussain 2. Sajjad Ahmad Khan 3. Inayat Ahmad 4. Nisar 5. Latif Ahmad	June 1990	After an exchange of fire with security personnel the five were taken to an interrogation centre.	An opposition group stated that they had been tortured to death.	
Mohammad Altaf Khan (28)	Between 20/05/90 and 23/05/90	Arrested on 20 May by the 268 Artillery Brigade and taken to Drugmula army camp.	Died reportedly of torture. His dead body was taken to hospital, 23 May. Army claimed he was shot in an encounter.	Post-mortem revealed that he had died as a result of head injuries and that his body was badly bruised. No bullet injuries found on his body.
Mohammad Ayub Khan (35)	14/05/90	Arrested 14 May by the 68 Mountain Brigade from his home.	Reportedly tortured during interrogation, then killed by five bullets fired at close range.	
Abdul Majid Khan (22)	May 1990	Arrested by the 68 Mountain Brigade on 22 May with his father, shot and injured. Taken for interrogation.	Several days later, body was found with an eye missing and numerous bruises and burns.	

Appendix I

Name, age, occupation	Date of death	Circumstances of arrest	Circumstances of death	Official action known
Shabir Ahmad Sulati (about 19)	May 1990	Arrested by the security forces and taken to an interrogation centre.	Died as a result of torture. His body was returned on 15 May by the police.	
Altaf Aly	May 1990	Detained mid-May with 14 others from Haihama-Payerpora, Kupwara district, by the security forces. Subjected to electric shocks.	The 14 other men were later released, but he was reportedly beaten to death in custody.	
A. Razak	07/04/90	Arrested by the armed forces in March.	Died due to torture during interrogation.	
Hilal Ahmad (early 20s)	Probably 1990	Arrested by the security forces in Kupwara and taken to an interrogation centre.	Died in custody. His body had one ear missing and burn marks.	
Sarabjit Singh (26)	08/06/89	Arrested 7 June by police in connection with a bank robbery.	Died following morning, reportedly due to torture. Official sources stated he committed suicide.	A magisterial inquiry ordered. The Minister of Works said those responsible had been discharged from duty and if found guilty they would be given fitting sentences.

India

Name, age, occupation	Date of death	Circumstances of arrest	Circumstances of death	Official action known
Ghulam Mohammad Shah (70)	05/04/89	Police claim he was taken into custody after he refused to hand over some people who had taken refuge in his house.	Died in hospital. Police say he had a cerebro-vascular attack and was taken to hospital immediately. One of his sons alleged that he had been "hit and severely beaten up by police".	
Ghulam Mohiuddin Ganai	October 1991		Died reportedly in interrogation centre after torture. Body handed over to police by security forces.	

Appendix I

Deaths in custody in Karnataka 1985 - 1991

Name, age, occupation	Date of death	Circumstances of arrest	Circumstances of death	Official action known
Channaiah	18/05/88	Arrested on suspicion of theft. Police said arrest was 17 May, wife claimed 12 May.	Found hanging in Subramanyanagar police station. Police claim suicide but opposition alleged he died from torture.	Post-mortem found death due to hanging. Opposition demanded second post-mortem and judicial inquiry. State government ordered inquiry by magistrate. Three policemen suspended.
Chandrashekhar Mandi, cleaner	17/02/88	Arrested at home.	Died in custody of Banahatti police, Bijapur District, on day of arrest. Police claimed died after epileptic attack. Family alleged was beaten to death.	Karnataka High Court admitted petition seeking CBI investigation, compensation and action against those responsible.
Gurumurthy (21)	13/01/88	Taken to Doddapete police station on 13 January. Co-prisoner allegedly witnessed Gurumurthy's legs burnt with tyres.	Died in Doddapete police station.	Police inquiry ordered: some police officials suspended and remanded in custody until 2 February. Minister promised compensation to family and judicial inquiry.

India

Name, age, occupation	Date of death	Circumstances of arrest	Circumstances of death	Official action known
Raj Kumar	13/01/88	Taken to Doddapete police station on 13 January. Co-prisoner claimed he was himself tortured with Raj Kumar and Gurumurthy (see above).	Died in custody of Doddapete police.	As in Gurumurthy's case (see above).
M. A. Rasheed (40), lawyer	18/08/87 (approx.)	Arrested 14 August by police from High Grounds, Bangalore, for trespassing. Released same day, he claimed he had been tortured. On 16 August he told Bangalore lawyer he had been rearrested for speaking to the press about his detention.	Found dead on railway lines near Salem in Tamil Nadu, two days after rearrest.	Injuries on body inflicted before death. CBI inquiry held police and former Karnataka home minister responsible. Trial on charges including murder referred to Madras High Court. Seven police officials were condemned to various terms of imprisonment, including two life sentences, for murder.
Narasimha Raju (20)	12/08/91	Arrested 8 July by Tilak Park police in connection with theft. Police later denied arrest.	Fellow prisoners claimed he was tortured and killed in police custody. Body found by roadside in Chikmagalur.	Post-mortem noted several injuries. Magisterial inquiry held. Police denied arrest and torture. Three police officers charged with illegal arrest, torture, murder and destroying evidence. Government reportedly granted Rs 20,000 relief.

Appendix I

Deaths in custody in Kerala, 1985 - 1991

Name, age, occupation	Date of death	Circumstances of arrest	Circumstances of death	Official action known
Balakrishnan Nair	10/07/89	Arrested 9 July in Neyyattinkara.	Found hanging in Neyyattinkara police station the next morning	Kerala Government reportedly announced a judicial inquiry. Two policemen suspended.
Thampi (26)	27/02/88	Arrested 26 February and taken to Cochin sub-jail.	Dead on arrival at hospital in Cochin. Police claimed he suffered an epileptic fit.	
Nasiruddin	15/02/86	A hospital patient, he reportedly assaulted a warden and was then beaten to death by hospital staff and duty police.	Died in Quilon District Hospital after being beaten unconscious.	Four Armed Reserve Police constables reportedly arrested.
Sasidharan Nair	14/12/85	Arrested 14 December on suspicion of theft. Taken to Vanchivoor police station, Trivandrum.	Allegedly beaten to death. Police claimed he hanged himself.	Judicial inquiry reportedly ordered by Kerala Government.
Manian	28/11/85	Arrested 20 November after a fight. Taken to Balarampuram police station. Released on bail next day, seriously injured	Taken to Medical College hospital, Balarampuram where he died.	Police reportedly registered a case against four police officials.

India

Name, age, occupation	Date of death	Circumstances of arrest	Circumstances of death	Official action known
Jose Sebastian	12/11/85	Arrested on suspicion of theft, 7 November. Not produced before magistrate.	Died in hospital. Doctor at Konni health centre said body bore signs of torture.	Four police officials remanded in custody on murder charges. Crime branch investigation attributed death to injuries; report passed to magistrate's court.
Velayudhan Pillai (58)	June 1991	Arrested 10 June by Forest Guards on suspicion of theft.	Body found 12 June near Karamana river, Trivandrum. He was allegedly beaten to death by police.	Post-mortem allegedly revealed marks of torture all over the body.
Kuttappam	04/07/91	Arrested on 3 July by Parassala police, Trivandrum. Allegedly beaten by a station constable.	Died on day of release allegedly as a result of torture by police.	Post-mortem reportedly revealed rupture of spleen caused by torture. Government reportedly suspended Sub-Inspector and a Constable. Police inquiry ordered.
Divakaram (46)	27/05/91	Arrested 23 May by Mannar police, Alapuzha district, for possession of cannabis. Brought to court 24 May, remanded to Mavelikara sub-jail.	Admitted to hospital on 27 May. Died same day, allegedly due to torture.	Post-mortem reportedly revealed signs of brain damage.

Appendix I

Name, age, occupation	Date of death	Circumstances of arrest	Circumstances of death	Official action known
Syamala Kumar	03/05/91	Arrested on 30 April by Trivandrum police, on charge of bootlegging. Allegedly beaten by police. Brought to court, 31 April, remanded to sub-jail.	Taken to hospital 3 May, where he died, allegedly due to police torture.	Post-mortem listed 10 injuries and contusions on body.
Madhavan Nair (62)	late July 1987	Arrested by Pathanamthitta police. Allegedly beaten by police officers, and returned to his house unconscious.	Died soon after being returned home, allegedly due to police torture.	
Rajendra-prasad (29)	end May 1989	Arrested late May by Trivandrum police. Allegedly tortured. Produced in court the day after arrest.	Died allegedly as a result of police torture.	

Deaths in custody in Madhya Pradesh, 1985 - 1991

Name, age, occupation	Date of death	Circumstances of arrest	Circumstances of death	Official action known
Wahid (also known as Ismail), (22)	21/09/89	Arrested by Omti police 20 September and held in Omti police station.	Police claimed suicide. Residents disbelieved this.	Post-mortem reportedly attributed death to suicide. A High Court judge ordered second post-mortem by forensic experts in Bhopal and first post-mortem report and relevant papers to be produced.
Chandra, tribal youth	21/06/89	Arrested for attacking a police constable and taken to Khamaria police station, Jabalpur.	Died on day of arrest. The DIG Jabalpur reportedly said death due to possible beating by police.	Five policemen reportedly suspended.
Mohammad Hanif (40), factory worker	06/08/88	Reportedly drunk when arrested.	Died in Ranjhi police station.	Magisterial inquiry ordered.
Kanshi Aharwal (45)	01/07/88	Arrested 30 June and taken to Banwar police post under Kumhari police station. Released next morning.	After release on bail, taken to hospital where died, allegedly due to beating in police custody.	Magisterial inquiry ordered.

Appendix I

Name, age, occupation	Date of death	Circumstances of arrest	Circumstances of death	Official action known
Kunjami Pandu	June 1988	Arrested on suspicion of murder. Allegedly severely beaten by police.	Died on way to hospital, having his throat cut in Bhairmagad police station.	Victim's fellow villagers demanded impartial inquiry.
Balwant Singh	13/05/88	Arrested 11 May and taken to Pichhore police station.	Found hanging from a tree, allegedly with visible wounds.	Post-mortem reportedly found death due to ruptured spleen. Four policemen reportedly dismissed and charged with murder.
Govardhan (55)	31/03/88	Arrested 16 March and held in Seraipali police station.	Died in D.K. Hospital.	
Krishna Masih (35)	16/02/88	Arrested on suspicion of selling liquor illegally. Taken to Chakarbhata police station where police claimed he fell ill with chest pain.	Taken by police to Bilsapur district hospital the day after arrest, where he died.	Inquiry carried out by Sub-Divisional Magistrate.
Pyarelal	1988	Took part in protests about jail conditions. According to other prisoners, he was subsequently beaten.	Died in hospital, allegedly due to beatings by guards of Kanker sub-jail.	State government reportedly asked for details of death.

India

Name, age, occupation	Date of death	Circumstances of arrest	Circumstances of death	Official action known
Ram Dayal	1988	Arrested with friend (who reportedly escaped); both beaten during arrest. Eye-witnesses said he was taken alive to police station where he was allegedly tortured.	Died either in Naugaon Hospital or Lugasi police station the day after arrest.	Post-mortem reportedly found 30 injuries including broken ribs. State home minister announced two policemen suspended and charged with murder. *Ex gratia* payment reportedly made to family.
Joga Rao	02/12/87	Arrested in Bhilai 1 December in connection with fraud, and held overnight.	On 2 December was admitted to hospital where he died, allegedly due to beating by police.	District officer reportedly said an inquiry would be held. Case taken up by several MLAs.
Achchhelal Joshi (55 or 60)	Dec. 1987	Arrested 13 December by Tikamgarh police. Allegedly beaten when unable to pay bribe.	Died in Tikamgarh police station soon after arrest.	Magisterial inquiry ordered. Family reportedly offered Rs2,000 compensation.
Tulsi Ram Kachi	25/08/87	Convicted for murder in 1977 and serving life sentence. Allegedly beaten for refusing to do forced labour.	Died in Sagar district jail, allegedly due to beating by police. Police claim death due to illness.	Apparently no post-mortem held. Opposition leaders demanded inquiry, but none is known to have been held.

Appendix I

Name, age, occupation	Date of death	Circumstances of arrest	Circumstances of death	Official action known
Sardar Singh	23/08/87	Held in jail since 4 August and died the day his case was to be heard.	Died in Sagar district jail, allegedly due to beating given because family did not pay bribe. Jail staff reportedly claimed death due to illness.	
Kamla Bai	05/08/87	Reportedly illegally detained on suspicion of theft. Tortured under interrogation.	Died in Padwara police station. PUCL investigation attributed death to beating by police.	Post-mortem carried out at Katni Hospital. Magisterial inquiry held. Sub-Inspector suspended.
Lakhan Singh	July 1987	Arrested in Bahroul village and questioned about theft. Family visited him for three days after arrest.	On fourth day body found in forest near police station. Family alleged he was killed by police.	Family asked for judicial inquiry.
Mihir Ahirvar	June 1987	Arrested 28 June in Karapur village, on drink charge.	Reportedly beaten all night and taken to hospital next day, where he died.	
Chaturbhuj Singh (60)	27/02/87	Arrested in January by Jabera police and allegedly kept in illegal detention and tortured for one month.	Found hanging from a tree.	State home minister announced inquiry by Inspector General of Police for Gwalior.

India

Name, age, occupation	Date of death	Circumstances of arrest	Circumstances of death	Official action known
Shivalingappa Shirol	Feb. 1986	Arrested 4 February. His wife complained to district Superintendent of Police (SP) that her husband had "disappeared".	Died in Mahalingapur police station.	SP instituted departmental inquiry which reportedly said death resulted from beating by Head Constable. SP recommended further inquiry.
Ghasiram Satnami	Jan. 1986	Arrested on suspicion of theft with wife who was reportedly stripped; both reportedly beaten.	Died in Malharoda police station, Bilaspur district, allegedly after beatings by police.	State home minister announced that case had been registered against some police officials, who had absconded.

Appendix I

Deaths in custody in Maharashtra, 1985 - 1991

Name, age, occupation	Date of death	Circumstances of arrest	Circumstances of death	Official action known
Arun Tulshiram Kharat	09/03/89	Arrested on suspicion of kidnapping and raping a minor on 8 March approx.	Died in Ghatkopar police station. Police claimed death due to suicide by hanging.	State home minister reportedly said an inquiry would be held. Some police officials were reportedly suspended.
Jagdish (also known as Jaggu) Laxman Chavan	03/03/89	Arrested 15 February by police from Palton Road police station, Bombay. Taken to Khopoli police station where he was beaten with 19 others. All accused of gang robbery.	Died in Panvel Hospital where he had been taken by police the day before. Body handed over to relatives (who say it was swollen and covered in contusions) and cremated.	Medical reports listed many injuries due to beating. Judicial inquiry found insufficient evidence to prove death was due to torture. Inquest held by executive magistrate.
Desharath Ashroo Patthe (32)	07/08/88	A suspended policeman, he was arrested on 4 August on suspicion of theft.	Died in J.J. Hospital where he was taken from Byculla police station on 7 August. Police claimed death due to alcoholism.	Coroner said death was due to alcohol withdrawal but alterations were reportedly made to both death certificate and post-mortem report.
Siddharth Taku Nage	10/06/88		Died in Tilak Hospital, Sion, allegedly due to assault the previous day in Jawahar Nagar, Khar (East) police station.	Constable from Nirmal Nagar police station arrested and charged with murder.

India

Name, age, occupation	Date of death	Circumstances of arrest	Circumstances of death	Official action known
Riyaz Sadik Varekar	09/06/88	Arrested by Mumbra police after a fight. Sent to Rabale police station, Thane.	Taken by police to Thane Hospital, where died, allegedly due to beating by police on 8 June.	Magisterial inquiry began immediately. State home minister said death due to "cardio-respiratory failure", and ordered a CID inquiry.
Sodarraj Thangraj (also known as Vadovelu), (24) civic employee	01/03/88	Arrested by Santa Cruz (West) police on 29 February on suspicion of theft. Taken to Santa Cruz police station.	Died in Cooper Hospital where was taken by police on day after arrest. Police reportedly admitted torture by a Santa Cruz constable.	Second post-mortem found death resulted from multiple injuries. State home minister announced CID inquiry. In October CID charged five people, including a Santa Cruz constable, with culpable homicide.
Prakash Ramchandra Kamble	11/11/87	Arrested 11 November with one other by Naupada police for possession of lethal weapons.	Died, allegedly due to severe beating by Thane police, soon after appearing before magistrate with blood oozing from his mouth. Co-accused reportedly witnessed torture.	Post-mortem found death due to "multiple injuries". Magistrate's inquest listed extensive external wounds. Inquiry ordered into why remanding magistrate had failed to file FIR after the death or to record evidence of co-accused and other witnesses.

Appendix I

Name, age, occupation	Date of death	Circumstances of arrest	Circumstances of death	Official action known
Suresh Dinkar Doiphode (also known as Bhurya)	11/03/87	Arrested by Subhanshah police at 11am, 11 March. Witnesses claimed police beat him.	At 1pm he was taken semi-conscious to Faraskhana police station. Reported dead 2pm. Police told relatives he had hanged himself. Body reportedly cremated by police immediately after post-mortem, before it had been seen by relatives.	Post-mortem carried out at Sasoon Hospital. State government appointed a commission to investigate; two police constables suspended.
Hushiara Singh	25/05/87	Three policemen from Hill Line police station searching for his brother, beat him until he collapsed.	Declared dead on arrival at Sarvanand Hospital Ulhasnagar where was taken by family.	Post-mortem said death was due to heart failure which could have been caused by chest injuries. Petition filed in Bombay High Court sought full inquiry.
Maruthi Dahikar	26/04/87 or 27/04/87		Died in Brahmapuri police station allegedly due to beating by a police inspector.	State home minister stated he committed suicide by hanging.
Balu Rambhau Kanhayye	02/02/86	Arrested with brother after communal riots. Eye-witnesses claimed the two were beaten with canes.	Died in Chopda police station, Jalgaon district, allegedly due to torture by police.	Fifteen police officials charged with murder. After three months were released on bail.
Murli Rambhau Kanhayye	02/02/86	As above (Balu Rambhau Kanhayye).		

141

India

Name, age, occupation	Date of death	Circumstances of arrest	Circumstances of death	Official action known
Vishwas Lotangane	29/08/90	Arrested with 16 others after the murder of a company manager. Allegedly beaten by police in custody. Held in Harsul jail under TADA.	Died in Harsul prison, allegedly as a result of torture.	
Nandalal Rughawani (19)	30/06/90	Allegedly arrested with his brother after a complaint by a neighbour.	Died in police custody allegedly due to police beatings.	The policemen involved in the arrest were suspended. A CID inquiry was announced. The minister of state for home affairs claimed the victim had cirrhosis of liver and congested lungs.
Vijendra-singh Thakur (19)	03/06/90	A prisoner in Wardha district jail, arrested in May 1990.	Died in Wardha district jail. Police claim he was mentally unbalanced and died after a fall.	Three policemen were reportedly suspended. An inquiry was ordered by the Inspector-General of Prisons.
Bhagwan Navle	20/05/90	Held in the custody of Hasnabad police in Jalna district.	Died in suspicious circumstances.	Three policemen suspended and the state CID was reported to be investigating.

Appendix I

Name, age, occupation	Date of death	Circumstances of arrest	Circumstances of death	Official action known
Sheikh Jam Zakir (16)	03/08/91	Held in Jensi Nagar police station, Aurangabad.	Died in police station, allegedly as a result of torture to extract confession.	A Minister of State reportedly stated he was beaten. CID investigation was announced, in addition to a magisterial inquiry. An inspector and three constables were reportedly suspended, arrested and charged with culpable homicide.
Raju Mohite (26), *dalit*	06/07/90	Arrested by police on 26 June in Nasik village in connection with a burglary. Taken to Bombay and remanded in custody twice before being discharged on 5 July. Probably detained in Shivira police station, Andheri, Bombay, allegedly incommunicado.	Died in hospital the day after his release, allegedly due to torture.	Post-mortem revealed injuries consistent with torture. After a preliminary inquiry by the Crime Branch Unit, seven policemen, including a Sub-Inspector, were arrested for causing injury to extract confession.

143

India

Name, age, occupation	Date of death	Circumstances of arrest	Circumstances of death	Official action known
Ramu Aba Bhandirge	03/11/88	Arrested in Shenawadi by Aundh police on 3 November on suspicion of selling drugs. His son claimed he witnessed him being beaten by police until he began vomiting blood and collapsed.	Died soon after release, allegedly as a result of beatings by police.	In August 1990 the Bombay High Court directed the state CID (Crime), Pune, to conduct an inquiry. The Court set aside a 1989 report conducted by the Satara Deputy Superintendent of Police, CID, which had found that he had died of natural causes.
Namdeo Atak (18), *adivasi*	22/06/90	Reportedly beaten when he tried to prevent a group of drunken policemen from taking his sister away on 21 June. They were both taken to Tulzapur station where Namdeo was allegedly beaten and his sister, who was pregnant, sexually assaulted.	Died in police custody, allegedly as a result of four hours of beatings.	Post-mortem found broken bones. All the policemen allegedly involved were suspended and a high-level CID inquiry was instituted. The Chief Minister admitted police responsibility but rejected demands for a judicial inquiry.
Netaji Bahu Lohar (25)	25/04/90	Arrested by Hupari police on 18 April in connection with theft. Allegedly beaten by police in Hupari police station.	Body found next day hanging in police station. Allegedly killed by police.	Four policemen arrested and ten charged with murder. Post-mortem found he died of suffocation.

Appendix I

Deaths in custody in Manipur, 1985 - 1991

Name, age, occupation	Date of death	Circumstances of arrest	Circumstances of death	Official action known
S. Joel	24/05/90 or 25/05/90	Arrested in Viewland, Ukhrul, by Assam Rifles, 23 May. Detained at 20 Assam Rifles HQ in Somsai.	Died in custody of Assam Rifles, allegedly "shot while trying to escape". Family doubt this because he could hardly walk when brought home during interrogation.	Body taken to Ukhrul police station on 25 May.
M. Tharthing	23/05/90	Taken from his home early on 23 May by Assam Rifles.	Reportedly tortured and shot same morning. Body taken to 20 Assam Rifles HQ, Somsai.	Body handed over to Ukhrul police station on 23 May.
V. S. Cheery, timber trader	03/05/90	Detained by Assam Rifles in Gamnong village on 2 May with two others.	All three men reportedly tortured in custody; Cheery died as a result.	Post-mortem carried out at Ukhrul.
Khaningpang	21/11/88	In custody of Assam Rifles along with Shimreiwung (see below). Both members of underground Socialist Council of Nagaland.	Reportedly "shot dead while trying to escape".	
Shimreiwung	21/11/88	See Khaningpang above.		

145

India

Name, age, occupation	Date of death	Circumstances of arrest	Circumstances of death	Official action known
M. Esou, gaonbura (clan leader)	between 10/08/87 and 12/08/87	Detained by Assam Rifles on 11 July. Held in Khongdei Junior High School.	Assam Rifles claim he was killed in crossfire. Eye-witnesses report he was badly beaten, then shot by Assam Rifles.	
R. Khova, gaonbura (clan leader)	between 10/08/87 and 12/08/87	Detained by Assam Rifles on 11 July in Khongdei village.	Assam Rifles claim he was killed in crossfire. Villagers say he was tortured and shot by Assam Rifles.	Post-mortem showed that he had been shot in the back.
R. Mathotmi, member of Ngari village authority	between 10/08/87 and 12/08/87	Arrested on 15 July by Assam Rifles. Held in Khongdei Khuman village.	Assam Rifles claim he was killed in crossfire. Local reports suggest he was detained and badly beaten, then shot by the Assam Rifles.	Post-mortem showed that he had been shot in the back and had an injury to the right elbow.
P. Rangkhiwo, Ngari village headman	between 10/08/87 and 12/08/87	Arrested on 15 July by the Assam Rifles. Before his death he was held in Khongdei Khuman village.	Assam Rifles claim he was killed in crossfire. His son saw him being beaten in custody of Assam Rifles.	
K. Sunai (65), gaonbura (clan leader)	between 10/08/87 and 12/08/87	Arrested by Assam Rifles on 11 July. Allowed to go home, but rearrested five days later. Held in Khongdei Junior High School.	Assam Rifles claim he was killed in crossfire. Evidence shows the he was tortured and shot by Assam Rifles.	Post-mortem indicated that he had been shot in the back.

Appendix I

Name, age, occupation	Date of death	Circumstances of arrest	Circumstances of death	Official action known
N. Thava, member of the Khongdei Khuman village authority	15/08/87	Detained by Assam Rifles on 11 July. Rearrested twice and detained in Khongdei Junior High School.	Assam Rifles claimed initially he committed suicide by hanging. Other accounts claim he was tortured.	Post-mortem found "death due to hanging. Suicidal in nature".
P. L. Ring, headmaster	07/08/87 or 08/08/87	Arrested on 10 July by Assam Rifles. Held in Khongdei Junior High School.	Assam Rifles claim was killed in crossfire. Other accounts suggest he was tortured and then shot by Assam Rifles.	Assam Rifles offered family Rs.3,000 as compensation. Gauhati High Court blamed death on Assam Rifles, and ordered Rs.20,000 be paid to the family.
B. Wa, gaonbura (clan leader)	07/08/87 or 08/08/87	See above.	See above.	See above.
L. Zamo, (65), headman of Khongdei Khuman	07/08/87 or 08/08/87	Arrested on 11 July by Assam Rifles. Held in Khongdei Junior High School.	Assam Rifles claim he was shot in "encounter" between them and NSCN. Others claim he was tortured and then shot by Assam Rifles.	
P. Sanglong, Chairman of Oinam village authority	28/07/87	Arrested by Assam Rifles on 10 July. Later released, but rearrested the next day.	Assam Rifles claim he was "shot while running away". Wife and others claim he was tortured and could hardly walk.	Assam Rifles offered the family Rs3,000 in compensation.

India

Name, age, occupation	Date of death	Circumstances of arrest	Circumstances of death	Official action known
Th Wakhoa, gaonbura (clan leader)	28/07/87	Detained by Assam Rifles on 10 July 1987.	Assam Rifles claim was "shot while running away". Villagers stated he was tortured by Assam Rifles and then shot.	Assam Rifles offered the family Rs3,000 as compensation.
Nashir Khan (26)	between 28/08/91 and 30/08/91	Arrested 28 August by Lilong police, reportedly on drugs charge. Reportedly taken back to his home the same day, his house searched and he was beaten by police, who returned later and said he had escaped.	Body found handcuffed by the Imphal river on 30 August, with visible injury marks. His wife claims he was tortured to death by police.	
N. Krishnamohon Singh (29)	between 29/07/91 and 02/08/91	Arrested by Kakching police on 29 July.	Body found in a lake in Kharungpat area on 2 August. Father believes that he was killed by police in custody.	An inquiry was ordered by a Sub-Divisional magistrate.

Appendix I

Name, age, occupation	Date of death	Circumstances of arrest	Circumstances of death	Official action known
Ning-houjam Angou Singh	28/01/89	Arrested on 28 January by Chandel police. According to police, he had chest pain and was taken to Chandel District Hospital.	Died in hospital, allegedly due to beatings by police.	An inquiry was initiated by the SDM Chandel but discontinued. The death certificate stated that the cause of death was internal injuries and that he was "brought dead" to the hospital. The Forensic Science Laboratory, Guwahati, stated death due to "shock from testicular pain sensation by blunt object". The family filed a murder case and a suit for compensation. The Chief Judicial Magistrate directed the police to investigate.

Deaths in custody in *New Delhi, 1985 - 1991*

Name, age, occupation	Date of death	Circumstances of arrest	Circumstances of death	Official action known
Ram Swaroop	02/02/91	Reportedly taken 29 January to R.K. Puram police station in connection with theft on 29 January.	Died in police station, allegedly as a result of police torture.	Two policemen including a Station House Officer were suspended.
Reshna, female	22/03/91	She was reportedly taken to Gokulpuri police station with other members of her family on a charge of murder.	Six police officers were reportedly caught throwing her body into a drain.	The Station House Officer and five junior colleagues were arrested and charged with murder.
Jagannath	10/05/91	Reportedly arrested 1 May by Lahori Gate police, charged with running a brothel.	Allegedly beaten by police. Taken to hospital and died 10 days later.	
Ram Vilas	11/07/91	Ordered to vacate his house by company guards and police, but refused and was beaten.	Reportedly beaten by police until unconscious. Taken to hospital but dead on arrival.	A Sub-Inspector from Adarsh Nagar police station was suspended.
Om Prakash	12/07/91	Reportedly taken to Timarpur police station after a fight.	Died in police station, allegedly as a result of police torture.	

Appendix I

Name, age, occupation	Date of death	Circumstances of arrest	Circumstances of death	Official action known
Rohtas (also known as Fauji)	31/08/91	An inmate of Tihar Central jail detained for over two years under the Terrorist and Disruptive Activities (Prevention) Act in connection with kidnapping.	Found hanging in his cell.	A Magistrate said suicide was not a certainty. A Magistrate's inquiry was to be carried out once the post-mortem results were obtained.
Jairam Singh	19/08/91	Arrested 18 August with his son by Patel Nagar police after his son allegedly stole a purse.	He died in Patel Nagar police station, allegedly as a result of police torture.	Post-mortem found death due to cumulated effect of injuries. Three police officers were suspended, arrested and charged with murder. Station House Officer transferred. A Magistrate conducted an inquiry. Also inquiry by crime branch of Delhi police.
Rajesh	07/09/91	Arrested with two others for fighting by the Sultanpuri police on 6 September.	He died in Sultanpuri police station, reportedly as a result of torture.	The two arrested with him were charged with his murder. A Magistrate concluded that he died of viral hepatitis, although had previously been declared fit.

151

India

Name, age, occupation	Date of death	Circumstances of arrest	Circumstances of death	Official action known
Joginder Pal Gupta	22/08/90	Detained at Model Town police station on 21 August.	Declared dead on arrival at Hindu Rao hospital. Police claimed he died of heart attack but his wife saw the body badly mutilated.	Police Commissioner ordered three police officials be transferred. A magisterial inquiry was ordered but results not known.
Mohammed Salim (25)	19/07/90	Arrested by East Delhi police in Jaipur on suspicion of offence. Police claim he committed suicide on seeing them.	Died in Jaipur as a result of burns. Residents of Krishna Nagar allege police instigated his death.	Additional Deputy Commissioner of Police, East Delhi, held inquiry.
Shammu Khan	June 1990	Arrested 1 June by Seemapuri police. Residents alleged police tortured him.	Released 2 June; died in Guru Tegh Bahadur hospital shortly afterwards.	Lieutenant Governor of Delhi ordered magisterial inquiry.
Yograj (30)	February 1990	Detained at Tihar Central Jail.	Police claim he died of tuberculosis. Declared dead on arrival at Deen Dayal hospital where he was brought by police posted at jail.	Police inquired into cause of death. Magisterial inquiry ordered.
Subhash Chand (35)	23/01/90	Held in Geeta Colony police lock-up.	Died in police lock-up, allegedly as a result of torture.	

Appendix I

Name, age, occupation	Date of death	Circumstances of arrest	Circumstances of death	Official action known
Om Prakash (25)	19/10/89	Arrested by police Geeta colony station on suspicion of kidnapping.	Police say he jumped from the roof of police station but eye-witness questioned whether he committed suicide.	Magisterial inquiry ordered. One police officer suspended.
Dr Manmohan Singh (37)	13/07/89	Arrested with Uttam Singh in October 1987 on drug charges. He was the only witness to death in custody of Uttam Singh a year later.	Died in his cell at Tihar Jail, his wife noticing his belly was swollen.	Post-mortem recorded several bruises and noted he could have died of injuries. Magisterial inquiry ordered.
Dinesh Kumar (26), trader	13/06/89	Arrested by police from Mangolpuri police station in connection with theft; allegedly tortured.	Died in police custody.	
Vijay Kumar (30), washerman	19/03/89	Arrested on 19 March by police from Welcome Colony police station.	Found the same day hanging by the neck from ceiling fan in police custody. Police claimed suicide; relatives say he was beaten to death.	Results of post-mortem not known. One policeman reportedly suspended; judicial inquiry ordered.
Ravi Narang	10/02/89	Arrested 8 February by officials of Directorate of Revenue Intelligence who could not explain why he died in their custody.	Declared dead on arrival at Safdarjung hospital. Relatives alleged he was tortured to death.	

153

India

Name, age, occupation	Date of death	Circumstances of arrest	Circumstances of death	Official action known
Sardar Singh (65)	17/12/88	Arrested with son on 16 December under Arms Act (for possessing a knife). Relatives claim he was tortured.	Found dead in Tilak Nagar police station the morning after arrest. According to police he died of a heart attack.	Assistant sub-inspector suspended pending inquiry but reinstated three days later.
Asha Ram, sweeper	06/10/88	Arrested after fight and taken to Trilokpuri police station, where police say he collapsed. Local residents alleged he was killed in custody.	Declared dead on admission to hospital day after arrest.	Magisterial inquiry ordered.
Ram Swaroop (50), migrant worker, *adivasi*	17/09/88	Arrested 16 September by police from Inderpuri police station. Tortured when refusing to work for police without pay. Torture witnessed by other detainees.	Died next morning in Inderpuri police station. Police removed his body in a jeep.	Inquiry by Vigilance Dept. of Delhi police. Police admitted he died of torture. Seven policemen were arrested.
Uttam Singh (50)	06/07/88	Arrested October 1987 with Manmohan Singh who alleged that Uttam singh died of medical neglect.	Found dead in Tihar Jail, reportedly examined at JP hospital a few days before his death.	

Appendix I

Name, age, occupation	Date of death	Circumstances of arrest	Circumstances of death	Official action known
Rattan Lal (55)	14/05/88	Arrested 13 May on suspicion of theft; taken to Lodhi police station.	Died in police station, due to loss of blood from a throat wound. Police claimed he stabbed himself with glass.	According to police post-mortem found "no other injuries on his body except the gash he got when he stabbed himself".
Azad (26)	April 1988	Arrested in Maliana in connection with murder; taken to Vivek Vihar police station.	Died in Guru Tegh Bahadur hospital. Doctors suspected poisoning.	Magistrate conducted inquiry but outcome unknown.
Shankar Duley (or Dalai), (19), goldsmith	25/02/88	Arrested with three others 23 February by Prasad Nagar police. Admitted to hospital on 25 February and beaten through the night.	Died next day at Ram Manohar Lohia hospital.	Results of post-mortem not known.
Mahinder Kumar	25/08/87	Arrested with Ram Kumar on 24 August by Vivek Vihar police in connection with a murder of a man. Ram Kumar described how both were tortured.	Died in JP hospital the day after arrest from multiple injuries resulting from torture.	Results of post-mortem not known. Seven policemen suspended. Magisterial inquiry ordered.
Mahir (22), rickshaw puller	24/08/87	Arrested 23 August for "hooliganism" and held in Welcome Colony police station.	Died of injuries the day after release. Police claim he died of fall after release; residents allege torture in custody.	

155

India

Name, age, occupation	Date of death	Circumstances of arrest	Circumstances of death	Official action known
Gajendra, *dalit*	13/07/87	Arrested 12 July. Held in police custody for six hours.	Died at home immediately after release. He told family he was tortured by police.	A member of the Delhi Metropolitan council demanded judicial inquiry.
Kamal	28/06/87	Arrested by police who claim residents beat him near Khera hospital. Father claim police beat him to death in custody.	Died in Lohia hospital shortly after arrrest.	Results of post-mortem unknown. Report withheld from family.
Brahmvati (23), female	27/11/86	Arrested by Haryana police 26 November in connection with murder of husband. Taken to Alimundi police station. Relatives allege she was tortured to death.	Died after police questioned her.	Results of post-mortem not known.
Dayal Singh (40), security guard	20/09/86	Arrested 15 September on suspicion of theft; held at Sriniwaspuri police station, where allegedly tortured.	Declared dead on arrival at AIIMS. Police claimed he died of tuberculosis.	Post-mortem listed no external injuries but second post-mortem found many injuries and swelling of the brain, indicating the use of blunt force. Inquest by magistrate found that death was due to torture. In February 1989 three policemen were arrested for murder.

Appendix I

Name, age, occupation	Date of death	Circumstances of arrest	Circumstances of death	Official action known
Gopi Ram (35), tongadriver	23/08/86	Arrested with nephew from his home on 22 August; taken to Patel Nagar police station, where both were allegedly tortured.	Died in Patel Nagar police station, according to police of alcohol poisoning. Relatives allege he was beaten to death.	Three policemen charged with murder. In 1988 the Supreme Court held that police attempted a cover-up, and ordered an independent investigation.
Suraj Singh (28), farmer	12/08/86 or 13/08/86	Arrested 7 or 12 August on theft charge; taken first to Shakapur then Ghandi Nagar police station.	found dead in Ghandi Nagar police station. Police said he hanged himself. Relatives say he was beaten to death.	Findings of post-mortem withheld from family. Magisterial inquiry ordered.
Kamal Singh	17/04/86	Arrested on suspicion of theft on 17 April; taken to health centre with severe injuries, which police said were inflicted before arrest.	Died in Lohia hospital where doctors recorded injuries due to blunt objects.	
Daljit Singh (27), driver	24/01/86	Arrested from home on 15 January; held at Der Nagar and Ashok police station on suspicion of harbouring Sikh extremists. Police claimed he was arrested on 21 January. Relatives saw him in custody with injuries of torture.	Died in JP hospital, allegedly of torture.	Post-mortem at JP hospital found cardiac arrest caused death but second post-mortem found contusion on body.

Name, age, occupation	Date of death	Circumstances of arrest	Circumstances of death	Official action known
Mohinder Pal Singh (32), Sikh, doctor	24/05/85	Arrested 22 May in Ludhiana and questioned by police from Karol Bagh police sation, Delhi. Press reported he was tortured to death.	Died in Karol Bagh police station. Police claimed he was arrested on 24 May and hanged himself in the toilet.	Magisterial inquiry ordered.
Mohinder Singh (also known as Khalsa), (32)	13/05/85	Arrested 12 May and interrogated by police from Desh Bandhu Gupta Road police station about bomb explosions in Delhi. Press reported he was tortured to death.	Died 13 May in or before being taken to hospital by police who say he died by hurting himself against wall of police station.	Post-mortem listed blunt injuries on body causing death. Magisterial inquiry ordered.

Appendix I

Deaths in custody in Orissa, 1985 - 1991

Name, age, occupation	Date of death	Circumstances of arrest	Circumstances of death	Official action known
Sudhir Samad (14)	20/08/89	Reportedly arrested in Hatibari near Rourkela on 19 August. Rourkela police said had released him after questioning.	Found dead by a roadside. Police allegedly held post-mortem and disposed of the body without informing relatives.	A Sub-Inspector and home guard from Rourkela suspended and second post-mortem ordered. Home guard reportedly admitted assaulting him during interrogation.
Ramarahi Ho Munda (25), adivasi	20/03/89	Detained in Karanjia police station, Mayurbhanj district.	Died in Karanjia police station.	A Sub-Inspector and Constable from police station suspended. State Chief Minister announced crime branch inquiry.
K. Pradhan, adivasi labourer	25/06/88	Detained in G. Udayagiri police station, Phulbani district, after an argument with his wife.	Allegedly beaten to death by police. Police claim he committed suicide by hanging.	Three policemen suspended.

India

Name, age, occupation	Date of death	Circumstances of arrest	Circumstances of death	Official action known
Subal Pallei	09/03/87		Died during interrogation at Udala police station, Mayurbhanj district.	State Chief Minister reportedly refused judicial inquiry as magisterial inquiry had already blamed four policemen. The four were suspended and charged with murder, and the crime branch was investigating.
Kashinath Nayak	03/05/85	Detained in Purivhat police station, Cuttack.	Assaulted by police at Purivhat police station on 3 May.	In August 1988 two policemen were reportedly sentenced to five and eight years' rigorous imprisonment for culpable homicide not amounting to murder.
Susil Bag	late September 1991	Arrested by Sasan and Jujomura police in connection with a murder. He was detained for three days and reportedly assaulted.	Died after being released, allegedly as a result of being beaten by the police.	Two police officers were suspended and the police registered a case of murder against them. Second post-mortem was ordered by the district administration.

Appendix I

Deaths in custody in Punjab, 1985 - 1991

Name, age, occupation	Date of death	Circumstances of arrest	Circumstances of death	Official action known
Manjit Singh (24), police constable	17/08/91	Arrested under TADA on 8 August. Charged with involvement in violent attacks, including the murder of a policeman.	Died in hospital after telling doctors he had been tortured. Police claimed he suffered from dysentry. Medical report allegedly noted a number of external injuries.	Inquest conducted. Several people told a magistrate that he died as a result of torture. Magistrate stayed cremation while allegation of torture was investigated.
Avtar Singh	Probably July 1991	Reportedly detained 26 July by Patiala police. Illegally detained in an interrogation centre at Patiala.	Reportedly died as a result of torture in Patiala police custody. Police allege he died in an encounter.	
Tarsem Singh member of Punjab home guards	15/05/91	Arrested 9 May, held at Civil Lines police station, Amritsar.	Police claim he fell ill and was taken to hospital. Others state he died as a result of torture.	Announced that action would be taken against five policemen and that a murder case would be registered.
1. Gurpreet Singh 2. Sohan Singh	05/02/91	Detained by police outside Dakha village on 31 January.	Reportedly killed on the outskirts of Dakha village while in police custody.	
Parwinder Singh Ropar	01/01/91	Arrested 31 December 1990 by the BSF and taken to Beco interrogation centre.	Reportedly received fatal injuries as a result of torture, and died the next day.	

India

Name, age, occupation	Date of death	Circumstances of arrest	Circumstances of death	Official action known
Sukhdev Singh (also known as Kaka), (22)	02/10/90	Jalandhar police raided Nandpur village on 1 October, looking for him.	Police reportedly beat him to death. Police denied his arrest and claimed that he poisoned himself.	Post-mortem recorded at least 10 injuries. Despite three summonses the police did not appear before magistrate's inquiry.
1. Harpal Singh (24) 2. Baljit Singh (20), students	14/06/90	Official sources alleged that the two men died in an armed encounter at Kotla Ajner.	Police claimed they shot in self-defence, and later that one committed suicide. Others claimed that they had been tortured and killed in custody.	Investigation by the Deputy Commissioner concluded that "death of the two was not in the ordinary course of an encounter". Officials recommended prosecution but the Director General of Police protested that this would demoralize the police force.
Karamjit Singh (24)	30/05/90 or 31/05/90	Reportedly abducted on 30 May.	The police registered a case of suicide. His father alleged he died from torture by the police or CRPF.	Post-mortem indicated he had a variety of external injuries.
Bahadur Singh (28)	28/02/90	He attended a protest and was allegedly hit by police on 26 February. He stated he had been tortured in police custody.	Found later semi-conscious. Police stated he died from alcohol.	A doctor found his legs paralyzed and considerable injuries.

Appendix I

Name, age, occupation	Date of death	Circumstances of arrest	Circumstances of death	Official action known
Raghbir Singh	19/07/89	Arrested 19 July and held in police post, Khassa.	Died allegedly from beatings by police.	Sub-Division Magistrate undertook an inquiry. Local police reportedly refused to give evidence.
Gurmit Singh Machaki	11/07/89	Arrested at Bombay airport in connection with terrorist crimes.	Died in police custody at Muktsar. An official said he was bitten by a snake.	
1. Sarbjit Kaur (13), 2. Salwinder Kaur (14)	Between 11/06/89 and 16/06/89	The two girls "disappeared" on 11 June.	Both girls were reportedly raped and then killed by two police officers. Bodies found on 16 June. The police alleged they committed suicide.	The Governor ordered the dismissal and prosecution of two police officers who were reportedly detained but no formal complaint had been registered due to "lack of evidence". It was reported that local police beat the girls' parents to make them confirm the police version.
Surinder Singh (22)	30/04/89	Arrested for questioning about Sikh groups on 24 April. Phillaur police denied he was in their custody.	His parents located him and secured his release but he had been badly tortured and died later.	

163

India

Name, age, occupation	Date of death	Circumstances of arrest	Circumstances of death	Official action known
Balraj Singh Raji	Between 29/03/89 and 15/04/89	Reportedly taken to Nurmahil police station on 29 March. Police allege he was arrested after an encounter on 15 April.	Died in custody, allegedly as a result of torture. Police initially denied arrest, then claimed that he committed suicide by taking poison.	The body was cremated before relatives could see it.
Balwinder Singh	06/11/89	Arrested on suspicion of links with Sikh groups. Remanded in police custody after being produced before a magistrate.	Reported to have committed suicide by hanging in police custody at Dhule.	
Inder Mohan Singh Uppal (also known as Simpy), (22)	12/09/88	Detained on the night of 11-12 September by CRPF and police personnel.	A police official reportedly claimed he had escaped and had not been arrested.	Case of kidnapping in order to murder was registered at Sarabha Nagar police station, Ludhiana. Investigation reportedly held.
Suresh Pal Singh, student	Between 10/02/88 and 17/02/88	Arrested 10 February. Taken to Bijoi police station.	Allegedly beaten to death by police. Police claimed he died from drinking.	An inquiry was ordered and a police official stated that the police responsible were being charged with manslaughter.
Gurbax Singh	02/12/87	Arrested 2 December in connection with a murder case.	Died in hospital after he reportedly complained of a chest pain.	Police inquiry was held. Post-mortem found he had 26 injuries and had died as a result.

Appendix I

Name, age, occupation	Date of death	Circumstances of arrest	Circumstances of death	Official action known
1. Wassan Singh, 2. Jagdish Singh Bhola, 3. Balwinder Singh	14/10/87	Prisoners held at Sangrur jail.	Three died and 27 were injured in shooting incidents in the jail. Officials claimed they fired in self-defence but others claimed the firing was unprovoked.	The Designate Court, Sangrur, directed the SHO, Kotwali Sangrur, to register an FIR and investigate the killings. Despite this order the SHO reportedly failed to register a case of murder. The SDM, Sangrur, was reported to have started an inquiry.
Sarbjit Singh Johal (21)	12/09/87	Arrested on 10 September in Amritsar.	Reportedly died due to police torture.	
Mukhtiar Singh	September 1986	Police stated he was wanted in connection with a shooting incident and was handed over to police on 19 August.	Allegedly tortured by Chheharta police. Police stated that he had a fever and died on the way home.	
Pramod Kumar	Between 02/03/86 and 14/03/86	Detained by two Sub-Inspectors and taken to Araghar police outpost for questioning on 2 March.	Died reportedly from injuries sustained during interrogation.	

165

India

Name, age, occupation	Date of death	Circumstances of arrest	Circumstances of death	Official action known
Gurinder Singh	10/05/85	Arrested following an encounter on 4 May in which he was alleged to have killed two police personnel. Reported to have been wanted in connection with the killing of a BJP leader in March.	Admitted to hospital with multiple injuries allegedly from torture. Police claimed these had been sustained during the encounter and arrest. He told doctors he was tortured after arrest.	An executive magistrate conducted an inquest and reportedly found that the injuries were "justified" as he resisted arrest.

Appendix I

Deaths in custody in Rajasthan, 1985 - 1990

Name, age, occupation	Date of death	Circumstances of arrest	Circumstances of death	Official action known
Lala Ram (teenager), bus conductor	12/06/90	Arrested by police in early June, allegedly in connection with a theft. Taken to a police station in Kotwali.	Died in police custody, reportedly as a result of being beaten.	A Minister stated he had been tortured to death by police. A Magistrate's report implicated two Sub-Inspectors and held the police station Officer-in-Charge guilty of negligence. A CID inquiry was ordered.
Banne Singh (50)	26/06/88	Arrested by Pushkar police on 25 June with two sons by Pushkar police.	Died in police custody on their way to hospital. Police claimed that residents lynched them; residents and a co-prisoner claim they were beaten to death by police.	A magisterial inquiry into the deaths was ordered in June; outcome not known. All 12 policemen in the Pushkar police station were suspended.
Mahendra Singh (28)	26/06/88	Arrested on 25 June by Pushkar police with two other family members.	As above.	As above.
Banne Singh (22)	26/06/88	As above.	As above.	As above.

India

Name, age, occupation	Date of death	Circumstances of arrest	Circumstances of death	Official action known
Mohan Singh	1985	Arrested by police in connection with theft.	Died in police custody after allegedly being beaten by police.	Criminal charges were brought against the police. State government offered Rs 1,000 to the widow, but a state legislator demanded a just amount. The Rajasthan government claimed "sovereign immunity" but lately agreed to pay Rs 30,000 "*ex gratia*".
Shyam Sunder Sharma	01/02/85	Beaten by Morak police during questioning.	Died in Kota hospital, allegedly of injuries sustained under police torture.	Post-mortem revealed he died of internal injuries.

Appendix I

Deaths in custody in Sikkim - 1988

Name, age occupation	Date of death	Circumstances of arrest	Circumstances of death	Official action known
Dharma Dhitta Sharma, Congress(I) party activist	12/02/88	Arrested by two policemen in Soreong on 12 February.	Beaten and killed by the two policemen. They reportedly dumped his body in Darjeeling district in West Bengal.	The two policemen were arrested and suspended but granted bail by High Court on 5 March 1988. State governor recommended investigation.

Deaths in custody in Tamil Nadu and Pondicherry, 1985 - 1991

Name, age, occupation	Date of death	Circumstances of arrest	Circumstances of death	Official action known
S. Bose, Deputy Organizer of Youth Wing of the DMK party	Feb. 1991	Arrested in Vilathikulam, Chidambaranar district, on 2 February.	Reported to have died in police custody as the result of beatings by the police.	Affidavit filed at Madras High Court on 7 February by local advocate contained details of death in custody.
G. Joseph (40)	17/01/91	Detained on 16 January at police station in Megnanapuram, Chidambaranar district.	Reportedly found hanged next morning.	A Head Constable and a Constable were suspended and the Tuticorin Revenue Divisional Officer conducted an inquiry.
Karmegam	14/01/91	Arrested on charges of creating disturbances and assaulting shop-keeper. Held at S.S. Colony police station.	Reportedly complained of a chest pain and died on the way to hospital.	Two Sub-Inspectors were suspended for not sending him to hospital and an inquiry by RDO ordered.
Ibrahim	Oct. 1990	Arrested in connection with theft of jewellery (found later to have been misplaced).	Family claimed he had crushed testicles, bruised forehead and wounds on his chest and stomach. Police said: "natural death".	

Appendix I

Name, age, occupation	Date of death	Circumstances of arrest	Circumstances of death	Official action known
Ashok Nagar (17), handicapped	Aug. 1990	Reportedly arrested for harassing women.	Beaten by police and died next day. Police claimed he died due to "chest pain".	
Ayyappan (also known as Mookan)	13/12/89	Reportedly detained on 27 November for theft. Held at Vaiyampatti police station, near Manapparai.	Reportedly found hanging from a tree inside Vaiyampatti police station. Allegedly tortured before death. Police said it was suicide.	Sub Collector conducted an inquiry. Three policemen were charged with murder and suspended. Second Additional Sessions Judge acquitted them on 1 November 1990.
Uthandi (35)	Dec. 1989	Arrested on charges of theft.	Found hanged in Cheyyur police station, near Maduranthakam.	Sub Collector reported to be holding a magisterial inquiry.
Vellaiyan	Oct. 1989	Arrested in connection with theft. Detained in Alanganallur police station, Maduria.	Police claim he escaped, committed suicide and that his body was found in nearby river bed. Local people alleged he died as a result of torture.	Policemen suspended and following inquiry by Madurai RDO, criminal proceedings were reportedly instigated against seven policemen.

India

Sekar (25) *dalit*, law student	02/09/89		Shot in leg by police in Panaiyadikuppam, Pondicherry, and then reportedly beaten to death by Tamil Nadu police. Police claim he was shot in Sorapur, Tamil Nadu, during rioting and died on the way to hospital.	Relatives refused to accept compensation because conditional on their confirmation of police version. Relatives had been denied access to post-mortem report.
Poovappan, farmer	May 1988	Arrested when police raided an illegal cockfight centre at Moodambail.	Reportedly beaten to death by police.	
V. Vellaichamy (38) a tea shop owner and DMK worker	15/03/88	Arrested on 12 March in connection with a strike.	Died in Tiruchi jail, reportedly suffocated due to overcrowding after arrest of some 40,000 during the strike.	Opposition members in the Rajya Sabha demanded judicial inquiry.
Paramasivam (20)	04/06/88	Arrested for "moving suspiciously".	Family told he died of "natural causes".	Post-mortem stated he had died of shock due to injury to his testicles.
K. Raman (27) washerman	Oct. 1987	Detained in connection with theft from Tamil Nadu Electricity Board.	Died in Thuvarankurichi police station. Reported to have electrocuted himself on lamp post of police station. Locals alleged that the police had driven him to suicide.	Deputy Superintendent of Police and Sub Collector went to police station and promised inquiry to demonstrating crowd.

Appendix I

Munusami and one other	24/09/87 and 23/09/87	Both were among 20,000 arrested in connection with agitation by the Vinnayars.	Munusami died in the Central Jail, Madras, the other in Coimbatore.
M. Kattaiyan (also known as Dakshinamurthy), *dalit*	Jan. 1987		Released the day after arrest and died the following day. Local residents took his body to the police station and claimed he had died from police torture.	Departmental inquiry was ordered.
Thiru Kathamuthu (24), AIYF activist and CPI worker	Dec. 1986	Detained in Dhanwantri Nagar police station in connection with theft.	Reportedly died from physical assault and then covered in kerosene and burned. Police claimed he set fire to himself.	Supreme Court order on 7 September 1989 ordered prosecution of the Station House Officer and constable of Dhanwantri Nagar police station and Rs25,000 interim compensation. Magisterial and CBI inquiry ordered; police constable reportedly suspended.
Sinthamani (also known as Arumugham), (33)	Sept. 1985	Police and revenue officials claim he was brought to Gingee police station on day of death. Others stated he was detained the previous night.	Died in Gingee police station. Reliable sources stated that there were external injuries on body.	Inquiry undertaken by Sub Collector.
Dhanushkodi	Sept. 1985	Arrested for jewel theft.	Reported to have committed suicide in Thevaram police station.	A Sub-Inspector and three Constables suspended for neglect of duty in connection with alleged suicide.

173

India

A. Vadivelu	1985	Detained in February 1985 by Wallajabad police in connection with double murder in Pullambakkam.	"Disappeared" after detention. Wife claimed he was tortured to death by the police.	In response to *habeas corpus* petition Madras High Court ordered Rs50,000 compensation in 1988. Court ordered Police to ask CID to register a case against the police allegedly involved.
Chinna-thambi (also known as Gnanasekaran), (37)	13/07/91	Arrested 10 July by police and sent to Central Jail in Tiruchirapalli.	Died in jail in suspicious circumstances.	

Appendix I

Deaths in custody in Uttar Pradesh, 1986 - 1991

Name, age, occupation	Date of death	Circumstances of arrest	Circumstances of death	Official action known
Masha Allah, rickshaw-puller	16/09/88	Arrested on 7 September by four policemen.	Died in T. P. Nagar police station, allegedly as a result of torture.	Four Sub-Inspectors, including Station House Officer of police station suspended. Orders for arrest issued.
Rajendra Prasad Sahu, trader	11/06/88	Arrested for possession of "illicit liquor" on 10 June and allegedly tortured by Sub-Inspector at Dhomanganj police station.	Died at a nursing home (or possibly before arrival), where he was taken by police.	Police allegedly disposed of body in secret, before informing relatives. *Ex gratia* payment of Rs25,000 made to family. District Magistrate ordered arrest of the Sub-Inspector on murder charge.
Darshan Sharma	June 1988	Arrested for non-payment of taxes and taken to Balrampur Tehsil lock-up.	Died the day after arrest.	State government ordered an inquiry.

Name, age, occupation	Date of death	Circumstances of arrest	Circumstances of death	Official action known
Jawahar Lal Gupta (35), shopkeeper	21/02/87	Arrested on 18 February (police claim 21 February) by Munderwa police in connection with robbery. Family allege torture during unacknowledged detention, 18-21 February.	Died in hospital of injuries. Police say he jumped under moving truck in Khalidabad, trying to escape. Relatives fear he was beaten to death and his body thrown under truck.	Post-mortem found wounds resulting from accident. Medico-legal expert found some injuries could have been caused by police torture. Magisterial inquiry found death was accidental. Illegal detention confirmed. CID found evidence of police interference with records, but no evidence that police had murdered him. State government granted Rs5,000 to wife and announced it would prosecute six policemen.
Gulsheer Ahmad	15/06/86	Arrested from home on day of death. Allegedly beaten at Khulabad police station.	Died of injuries in Tej Bhadur Sapru Hospital.	
Virendra Bahadur Singh	14/06/86	Taken from home on 9 June and interrogated for six days at Bakshi-ka-Talab police station, Lucknow district.	Died in custody. Police reportedly disposed of body and denied arrest.	

Appendix I

Name, age, occupation	Date of death	Circumstances of arrest	Circumstances of death	Official action known
Ganesh Singh, primary school teacher	11/05/86	Arrested on 8 May by Vrindaban police, in connection with kidnapping. On 9 May he was reportedly seen at Govardhan police station and said he feared police were plotting to murder him.	Police told family he had jumped from a train en route to Agra for further questioning.	
Bhagwati	18/04/86	Arrested on murder charge.	Died in custody of Jagatpur police, Rae Bareli district.	
Garib Ram, landless labourer	06/02/86	Police claimed he had been arrested on suspicion of dacoity in Mishrawaliyan, taken to hospital complaining of abdominal pain and had "died a natural death".	Allegedly tortured 5 February by Gahmar police. Died after admission to hospital. Police reportedly tried to make family cremate the body without post-mortem.	
Drigpal	Feb. 1986	Arrested on charge of rape. Severely beaten at Madnapur post of Tihhar police station, Shahjaanpur district.	Died soon after he was sent to prison, allegedly from injuries caused by torture.	
Motilal *dalit*	08/01/86	Held in Khampar police station, Deoria district.	Allegedly tortured to death in police station and later falsely implicated in theft.	

India

Name, age, occupation	Date of death	Circumstances of arrest	Circumstances of death	Official action known
Munna rickshaw-puller	Jan. 1986		Reportedly beaten to death by Ghazipur police.	
Ganju Singh	June or July 1989	Arrested the day before death on suspicion of theft. Taken to Muffasil police station.	Police reportedly tortured him to death, disposed of body and denied arrest.	
Kuber Lal	05/08/91	Arrested by Sandila police on 26 July. Allegedly beaten by police in Hardoi jail. Visited on 28 July by a member of the legislative assembly and doctor who urged hospitalization.	Died in Hardoi jail, allegedly due to police torture and medical negligence by prison authorities.	Parliamentary Affairs Minister announced a magisterial inquiry. MLAs requested a high-level inquiry.
Four prisoners	22/10/91		Four men died in hospital from being poisoned, reportedly by officers of Fatehpur lock-up.	Head Constable of Fatehpur lock-up suspended. The Circle Officer of Khaga reportedly initiated an investigation.
Rahisuddin (14)	08/10/91	Taken to Dadri police station by members of public on 18 September. Police claim he was beaten by those who apprehended him, others allege he was beaten to death by police.	Died either in hospital or in Dadri police station, allegedly due to torture.	Magisterial inquiry ordered.

Appendix I

Name, age, occupation	Date of death	Circumstances of arrest	Circumstances of death	Official action known
Jamil Ahmed Dariwala (47)	25/05/87 or 26/05/87	Reportedly arrested by the Provincial Armed Constabulary on 22 May and allegedly beaten at the Meerut police lines. Taken to Fatehgarh Jail, 24 May.	Died in Fatehgarh Jail, allegedly as a result of beatings by the police and the PAC.	Six other people died in same week in Fatehgarh Jail. Magisterial inquiry found six people died as a result of injuries received, among other places, "inside the jail" where "scuffles" took place. Four jail officials suspended, departmental proceedings launched against three other officials and three murder cases were filed.
Mohammed Hanif	25/05/87 or 26/05/87	Reportedly taken on 22 May to the Meerut police lines during riots, then to Thana Civil Lines and then to Fatehgarh Jail on 27 May.	See above.	See above.
Salim Siddiqui	25/05/87 or 26/05/87	See above.	See above.	See above.

India

Name, age, occupation	Date of death	Circumstances of arrest	Circumstances of death	Official action known
Deen Mohammed (early 20s)	25/05/87 or 26/05/87	See above.	Died in Fatehgarh jail, allegedly as a result of torture by the police and the PAC. His father was called to the jail on 29 May and ordered to bury the body before dawn.	See above.
Mohammed Osman	25/05/87 or 26/05/87	See above.	Died in Fatehgarh jail, allegedly as a result of torture by the police and the PAC.	See above.
Naresh (22)	early April 1988	Reportedly arrested 5 April with brother Rakesh (16) in Kanpur by Fatehpur police.	Police claim he was killed in an "armed encounter" near Silmi village, Fatehpur district, where his body was found. Body of brother never found.	A former minister visited Silmi village. The residents denied any encounter or exchange of fire had taken place there.
1. Moinuddin 2. Zaheer Ahmad 3. Meeno (also known as Moinnuddin)	22/05/87	Arrested by police and PAC on 22 May and taken to police lines where they were allegedly beaten.	Died on the way to Fatehgarh jail, allegedly as a result of beatings. Police originally denied arrests and beatings.	Several people have filed affidavits stating they witnessed the arrests and that the PAC beat the men until they lost consciousness.
Shabuddin, farmer	03/08/90	Arrested by Roda police in Encholi, near Mazaffarnagar and allegedly beaten.	Died reportedly as a result of police torture.	Four policemen were suspended and arrested.

Appendix I

Name, age, occupation	Date of death	Circumstances of arrest	Circumstances of death	Official action known
1. Qadir (50) 2. Haji Shamin (45) 3. Mohammed Yasin (65) 4. Mohammed Naim (30) 5. Ashraf (20) 6. Qamaruddin (22) 7. Iqbal Urf Balo (20) 8. Siraj Ahmed (22) 9. Jawaid (13) 10. Haji Mustaqeem (55) 11. Naim Ahmed (15) 12. Islamuddin (21) 13. Ayyub (18) 14. Qayyum (14) 15. Mohammed Younus (15) 16. Allauddin (16)	22/05/87	Arrested in Hashimpura by police and PAC on 22 May during communal riots. Over 600 people were allegedly arrested during curfew.	Reportedly taken at about 8pm on 22 May by truck to Murad Nagar, Ghaziabad district, shot and their bodies thrown into the Upper Ganga canal. Two of the five survivors have testified that they were taken to the canal by uniformed men identified as the PAC.	Inquiries carried out by the CBI, CID and by the Gian Prakash Committee. The committee's report was never published. The press reported that it "confirmed 40-60 youths were indeed taken from Hashimpura area in PAC trucks and were since untraceable." The government claimed that *ex-gratia* payment of Rs 20,000 was made to the relatives of 13 victims whose bodies were identified by their clothing. The families of the remaining 19 were also reportedly given such payment although their bodies have not been found. The government did not accept official responsibility for these killings.

India

Name, age, occupation	Date of death	Circumstances of arrest	Circumstances of death	Official action known
17. Akeel (18) 18. Akhalaque (45) 19. Mehtab (20) 20. Sadaruddin (40) 21. Nizamuddin (16) 22. Asif (19) 23. Jamshed (18) 24. Shamshed (14) 25. Abdul Haque (24) 26. Rizwan (22) 27. Naim (12) 28. Munna (40) 29. Hanif (32) 30. Mohammed Naseem (17) 31. Mohammed Yousuf (24) 32. Mohammed Shakir (18)	As above.	As above.	As above.	As above.

Appendix I

Deaths in custody in West Bengal, 1985 - 1991

Name, age, occupation	Date of death	Circumstances of arrest	Circumstances of death	Official action known
Saiful Sardar (18)	11/10/90	Arrested on 10 October on charge of theft. Taken to Khalbar police camp at Merrigunj).	Found dead in Kultoli police station, South 24-Parganas district on 11 October.	
Subhash Das (35)	10/09/90	Police stated he was illicit liquor dealer and had been arrested on 9 September.	Died in Ultadanga police station.	Body reportedly sent for post-mortem; Deputy Commissioner claimed there were no marks of external injury.
Ramchandra Marma (28)	16/04/90	Arrested on 15 April at Kalabani village after a fight.	Died in Jhargram police station. District Superintendent of Police said it was suicide.	
Bhola Kotal (26)	April 1990	Arrested in connection with theft.	Died in Fulbagan police station. Police alleged he committed suicide by hanging. Others said body was swollen and there were signs of profuse bleeding from the ears.	

India

Name, age, occupation	Date of death	Circumstances of arrest	Circumstances of death	Official action known
Ponkoj Chatterjee	Probably 1990		Reportedly died of injuries in airport police station. Police claim he died after public assault.	
Sankar Garai (35)	03/11/89	Police said he was arrested for unruly behaviour at Esplanade Metro stadium, Calcutta, on 3 November.	Police allege he committed suicide by hanging in Hare Street police station.	
Yusuf Molla, Congress(I) supporter	31/08/89	Arrested 13 August, reportedly in connection with gang robbery. Held at Kulpi police station.	He was reportedly found hanging; opposition said he had been beaten to death by police.	
Swapan Das (14)	25/07/89	Taken into custody of the Thakurpukur police on 24 July.	Found hanging in unfinished building in Calcutta.	Special Branch officer arrested on 25 July and charged with murder.
Sheikh Babu (45)	25/07/89	Arrested 23 July on suspicion of theft. Transferred to Kharagpur Sadar Hospital on 25 July, after being held at Kharagpur Town police station.	Died after admission to hospital, allegedly as a result of torture.	Sub-Divisional Officer reportedly conducted an inquiry.

Appendix I

Name, age, occupation	Date of death	Circumstances of arrest	Circumstances of death	Official action known
Matiar Rahman Gazi (50) Communist Party of India activist	03/05/89	Arrested on 2 May in connection with a gang robbery and taken to Hasnabad police station.	Declared dead on arrival at Basirhat hospital. Police stated he died of injuries sustained while trying to escape from a moving van. Others allege he died as a result of torture.	Post-mortem reportedly ascribed the death to cardiac problems. Inquiries conducted by Deputy Inspector General and CID. Murder charge filed against Officer in Charge at police station. Chief Judicial Magistrate found that police had tampered with records.
Raj Kumar Malla (22)	10/11/88	Arrested around 8 November in connection with forgery. Taken to CBI office, Calcutta, on 10 November for interrogation.	Fell from ninth floor of CBI office. Declared dead on arrival at SSKM Hospital.	Magisterial inquiry ordered. Police investigating allegations of 'foulplay'.
Sakil Ahmed (30)	07/11/88	Arrested on 6 November for disorderly conduct in Hatibagan Road, Beniapukur.	Taken from Beniapukur police station to Chittaranjan Hospital. Declared dead.	Magisterial inquiry ordered.
Jiten Halder (55)	18/10/88		Died in Basanti police station, allegedly as a result of torture.	

185

India

Name, age, occupation	Date of death	Circumstances of arrest	Circumstances of death	Official action known
Hemalata (female), servant	23/09/88		Died in Barasat police station. Police claim she tried to commit suicide but a press investigation alleged she died after torture.	
Prabir Debnath, owner of a cloth shop	06/09/88	Police alleged he was a drug addict. Arrested on charge of theft.	Died in Amherst Street police station, Calcutta. Police claim he committed suicide by hanging but family alleged he was tortured.	Police were reported to have obstructed relatives' investigations of death.
Purne Ghatra, member of the Gorkhaland National Liberation Front	21/08/88 or 22/08/88	Arrested by Central Reserve Police Force in Dooars, Jalpaiguri district, on 21 August on charges of holding up a truck.	A senior police official stated he died in custody from injuries sustained in a scuffle with police.	
Binay Kumar (38), Communist party of India (Marxist) supporter	19/08/88	He and his son were arrested on 19 August in connection with a theft.	Both men were reportedly beaten in Chandannagor police station.	Four policemen were reportedly suspended and a departmental inquiry ordered.
Gopal Singh (24)	20/07/88	Arrested for attempted theft.	Found dead in Jadavpur police station. Police alleged he died of beatings by local residents.	

Appendix I

Name, age, occupation	Date of death	Circumstances of arrest	Circumstances of death	Official action known
Madan Singh member of Centre of Indian Trade Unions	17/06/88		Died in police custody in Mahestala police station. Police stated he committed suicide; local people allege he was beaten to death.	
Kunreram Bauri	26/05/88	Arrested on 25 May in connection with theft and held in Andal police station.	Died in Bidhannagar Hospital, Durgapur. Police claimed he died as he tried to escape from a police jeep.	
Subhankar Sarangi, student	May or June 1988	Arrested in connection with a theft.	Reportedly tortured in Gopibhallapur police station, treated by doctor, discharged and tortured again. Died in Jhargram Hospital.	Post-mortem stated death caused by severe injury to head and ribs. Family initiated criminal proceedings against a police inspector in Gopibhallavpur, who was reportedly transferred to Jhargram.
Dhiren Hansda, adivasi youth	13/02/88		Reportedly died in Rajnagar police station, Birbhum. Police alleged he committed suicide.	

India

Name, age, occupation	Date of death	Circumstances of arrest	Circumstances of death	Official action known
Acharya Ajitananda Avadhuta (28), monk of Ananda Marg and school principal	24/01/88	Arrested 17 January, taken to Siliguri police station and allegedly beaten under interrogation about a bomb explosion.	Found dead in Siliguri police station, allegedly as a result of torture. Police made contradictory claims: he had died of poisoning and had committed suicide.	A magisterial inquiry was ordered.
Joydev Pramanick (32)	17/01/88	Arrested in connection with theft and taken to Tiljala police station for interrogation.	Found hanging in police station. Police alleged he hanged himself.	Deputy Inspector General and Superintendent of Police visited police station on 18 January.
Kartik Mohanty	26/12/87	Reportedly a convicted prisoner.	Died in custody of Moynapur police, Jalpaiguri. Police allege he jumped from a jeep.	
Ganesh Sinha	30/10/87	Arrested on 15 October in connection with a robbery.	On 29 October he was produced before the Sub-Divisional Judicial Magistrate, who sent him to jail. Died next day in Dum Dum Central Jail.	Inquiry revealed that Amdanga police had beaten him on 29 October before producing him before magistrate. Director General of Police asked to take action against policemen responsible.

Appendix I

Name, age, occupation	Date of death	Circumstances of arrest	Circumstances of death	Official action known
Manohar Jaiswal (22)	24/10/87	Arrested on 23 October in connection with a theft and held in Jorasanko police station.	Body found on a road; died later in Vishudhananda Hospital. Police alleged he had been assaulted by miscreants, but others claimed police tortured him.	Inquiries by Deputy Commissioner (Central) and Deputy Commissioner (Detective Department) led to suspension of two Sub-Inspectors and three Constables but no action against the Officer-in-Charge.
Nagen Kolay (also known as Nagendra), (60)	21/10/87	Arrested with one other on charges of immoral traffic in women on 21 October.	Both men were allegedly beaten in Keshpur police station, Midnapore district, resulting in Kolay's death.	The Director General of Police asked the Special Inspector General to conduct an inquiry. Post-mortem allegedly found many injuries.
Probash Kolay (55)	19/10/87	Arrested on 16 October on suspicion of theft. Produced in court and remanded in police custody for further interrogation.	Reportedly beaten regularly for three days in Lalbazar police station. Transferred to the Medical College Hospital, declared dead.	The inquiry report stated that he had not been tortured and that the body bore marks of old injuries, not necessarily the result of physical assault.
Mohammed Sheikh Alauddin (21)	19/09/87	Arrested on 19 September by Taltala police on charges including extortion.	Died in custody of Taltala police. Taken to Calcutta Medical College Hospital, declared dead on arrival. Police said he died of injuries from being beaten by local people before arrest.	The Police Commissioner sought a report from the Deputy Commissioner (Central).

India

Name, age, occupation	Date of death	Circumstances of arrest	Circumstances of death	Official action known
John Mondal	18/09/87	Wanted in connection with gang robberies. Reportedly arrested on 17 September from South 24-Parganas. Taken to Entally police station, and then to Lalbazar central police station.	Officials claim he was murdered by associates. Reports suggest he died in police custody after being beaten and/or falling ill.	The Joint Commissioner of Police Organization reportedly conducted an inquiry.
Seikh Jamal	31/07/87	Arrested by Government Railway Police, Shalimar, on 30 July in Birsibpur. Taken to Satragacchi police station in Howrah.	Died in Satragacchi police station. Police claimed he died of a "certain mysterious disease", but sources believed he was beaten to death.	An executive magistrate and the Superintendent of Railway Police asked to investigate. The Director General of State Police criticized Superintendent of Railway Police for "submitting a false report".
Samsul Haq	08/05/87	Reportedly arrested on 6 May in connection with robberies. Police said he was a "drug addict" and showed withdrawal symptoms while in Shyampukur police station.	A senior police official said he had been taken to Jorabagan police station for "some formalities" on his way to court. There he collapsed and died.	
Lakshman Sardar	15/11/86 (approx.)	Arrested on a murder charge.	Found hanging in Koichun police lock-up in the Mongolkot area of Burdwan.	

Appendix I

Name, age, occupation	Date of death	Circumstances of arrest	Circumstances of death	Official action known
Samir Naksar (17)	10/07/86	Arrested 10 July and taken to Kanthaltala police camp. Mother reportedly chased away from police camp when she went to inquire about her son.	Police claim he died of natural causes. Declared dead at Baruipur Hospital. Local residents said he was beaten to death for involvement in a petition about police inaction against local crime.	An inquest was conducted by executive magistrate. Inquiry was reportedly conducted by an Additional Superintendent of Police.
Baidyanath Ram (also known as Ramu), (25) servant	17/06/86 or 27/06/86	Arrested in connection with theft. Died same day.	Died in Jorabagan police station. Deputy Commissioner (North) said he died "as he slipped from the stairs in the police station", but admitted that the body bore marks of external injury.	
Lalji Hariji Mochi (70)	26/06/86	Brought from Rajkot by Gujarat police, to appear before Calcutta High Court.	Died in Lalbazar central police station, Calcutta. Police reportedly claim he suffered from asthma and died despite medical treatment.	The Police Commissioner ordered police inquiry.
Sheikh Anwar Ali Mollah (22)	21/04/86	Reportedly arrested on 20 April for theft. Taken to Jadavpur police station.	Police said he was beaten by a mob after the alleged theft and died from his injuries. Relatives claim he was beaten to death by police.	The Deputy Inspector General, Presidency Division, conducted inquiry.

India

Name, age, occupation	Date of death	Circumstances of arrest	Circumstances of death	Official action known
Akbar Mondal	January or February 1986	Reportedly arrested in January or February from Keorapara in connection with robbery. Taken to Lalbazar police station from Sealdah court.	Found hanging in Lalbazar police station. Police Commissioner claimed he committed suicide.	Inquiry by the Detective Department stated he "had committed suicide and the post-mortem report had confirmed it".
Kaniklal Mahato	04/01/86	Arrested with two others who were released upon payment of bribe. Detained in Howrah police station.	Doctor at Howrah Hospital said he was brought dead to the hospital on 4 January. Died allegedly of police torture.	Police stated that he died of epilepsy. A state Minister alleged that police had refused to record an FIR so that no case against police could be filed.
Aziz Khan (17)	10/12/85	Arrested in connection with an armed clash. Held at Karaya police station.	Died at Chittaranjan Hospital.	Post-mortem attributed death to multiple injuries. Deputy Commissioner (South) conducted inquiry and found that he had been "viciously roughed up by two constables who were under the influence of alcohol". Officer-in-Charge at police station was suspended. One constable arrested.
Kalu (17)	December 1985		Reportedly died after being tortured by police.	

Appendix I

Name, age, occupation	Date of death	Circumstances of arrest	Circumstances of death	Official action known
Apurba, youth prisoner	April 1985		Reportedly died after being tortured by police at Amta police station.	

INDIA

APPENDIX II

India: background

India is a secular parliamentary democracy with a federal structure. There are two houses of parliament, the *Lok Sabha* (House of the People), elected by adult suffrage, and the *Rajya Sabha* (Council of States), which is indirectly elected. India's union government is responsible for issues such as the budget, foreign affairs, defence, banking and currency. The 25 state governments are responsible for public order, police, the administration of justice and prisons.

India became independent from British colonial rule in August 1947. The Congress party ruled India for 30 years without interruption until its electoral defeat after the 1975-77 state of emergency proclaimed by Indira Gandhi. During the emergency there were large-scale human rights violations, including the detention of thousands of prisoners of conscience. Between 1977 and 1980 the Janata Dal party formed a coalition government. The collapse of this coalition was followed by another lengthy period of Congress party rule.

Elections in November 1989 led to a period of political instability. The Janata Dal party, led by V. P. Singh, formed a minority government which was forced to resign after a year. A breakaway faction from the Janata Dal party, the Janata Dal (Socialist) party led by Chandra Shekhar, formed a new minority government heavily dependent on the support of the Congress party. It in turn resigned in early 1991.

In May 1991, part way through the subsequent recent election campaign, former Congress Prime Minister Rajiv Gandhi was assassinated, allegedly by Tamil militants from Sri Lanka. The Congress party won the largest number of seats (226 out of 545) and the new Congress party leader, Narasimha Rao, became Prime Minister forming a minority government. The Bharatiya Janata Party (BJP), led by Lal Kishan Advani, became the official opposition in the *Lok Sabha* doubling its representation to 119 seats while the Janata Dal and the other main left-wing parties, the Communist Party of India (CPI) and the Communist Party of India (Marxist) (CPI (M)), suffered a decline in support. These left-wing parties now control less than a fifth of seats in the *Lok Sabha*.

In November 1991, 15 parliamentary by-elections were held. Although the Congress party won more seats than any other party, it still does not command a majority in the *Lok Sabha*.

The Congress party also controls the majority of state assemblies, but many states are ruled by different parties from those in power at the centre. National opposition parties have regional strongholds —the CPI (M) has ruled West Bengal since 1977, and the BJP now controls four northern states in the traditional 'Hindi' belt — while in other states, especially in the south, regionally based parties hold power. In Tamil Nadu the All India Dravida Munnetra Kazhagam (AIADMK) controls the majority of seats in the state assembly, and governs in alliance with the Congress party.

APPENDIX III

Amnesty International's work on India

Amnesty International was not in existence to oppose the detention of numerous campaigners — notably Mahatma Gandhi and Jawaharlal Nehru — who peacefully struggled to achieve independence. They embody the very essence of the idea of a prisoner of conscience, whose imprisonment Amnesty International was created to oppose.

Amnesty International was founded in 1961 and has since worked to improve human rights protection all over the world. One of the first prisoners of conscience in India for whose release Amnesty International campaigned was Sheikh Muhammad Abdullah, the former Kashmir Prime Minister, detained almost continuously between 1953 and 1968 for peacefully advocating Kashmir's right to determine its own future. During the 1975-1977 emergency, Amnesty International mounted a world-wide campaign to urge the release of thousands of prisoners of conscience from all walks of life and political persuasions. They were detained without charge or trial for their views or beliefs and were even denied the remedy of *habeas corpus*. After that, Amnesty International visited India in January 1978 to discuss with the Janata Dal government structural measures for long-term human rights protection. It was the first and last Amnesty International delegation which visited India to have substantive discussions of its concerns with the government and to be permitted to carry out research in the country.

Amnesty International published its first report on India in 1974: it analyzed detention conditions in West Bengal jails. Amnesty International has since published numerous reports dealing with specific aspects of its human rights concerns. These are the detention without charge or trial of several thousand political prisoners each year, some of whom are prisoners of conscience, the systematic use of torture, dozens of "disappearances" and extrajudicial executions of peaceful demonstrators and political activists in "encounters" with the police. It is also concerned about the continued use of the death penalty.

Major reports published include one on long-term detention of political suspects from Punjab, an analysis of special laws curbing human rights, a study on the death penalty, a review of caste related human rights violations in Bihar and a case study of torture and extrajudicial executions perpetrated by the army in northeast India. More recently, two reports on the use and abuse of the law in Punjab were published. In addition, Amnesty International has issued numerous appeals to prevent executions of criminal and political prisoners, and to condemn extrajudicial executions, especially in Jammu and Kashmir, while pressing for justice for the victims. It has repeatedly stated its condemnation of torture and killing of prisoners — including hostage-taking — by anyone, including armed groups who oppose the government.

This report focuses on the pervasive use of torture, one particular form of human rights violations which is of grave and long-standing concern to many Indians and to Amnesty International.